THE *REAL* NEW ECONOMY

By:

Douglas N. Thompson
Garry K. Ottosen

Published by Crossroads Research Institute, a nonprofit
operating foundation conducting research
on economic issues.

Crossroads Research Institute
50 South Main Street, Suite 1090
Salt Lake City, Utah 84144

ISBN: 0-9624038-2-2

CONTENTS

CHAPTERS   **PAGE**

Introduction : What Is the *Real*
New Economy?   1

1. The Changing *Nature* of Competition
   and Its Impact on Productivity   4

2. The Changing *Intensity* of Competition
   and Its Impact on Productivity   14

3. Two Special Aspects of the Competition-
   Productivity Relationship   23

4. Competition and Unemployment   30

5. History of Structural and Below-Capacity
   Competition Since World War II   46

6. New Economy Policy Requirements
   for the United States   59

7. The Long-Term Outlook for the
   New Economy   63

8. New Economy Stock Valuations   86

WHAT IS
THE *REAL* NEW ECONOMY?

The term *New Economy* has often been spoken with derision since the bubble years when it was so badly used. But we do, indeed, have a New Economy, a *real* New Economy. It is not a sickly development based on stock speculation and Internet hype. It is an exciting new opening based on powerful forces that have strengthened throughout the last half century and especially during the past two decades. This report is directed toward describing the workings of that New Economy.

Much that has been written about the New Economy starts with the assumption that it is a product of the information technology (IT) revolution. That is backwards. The IT revolution is just one of the products of the New Economy. And the New Economy is, in turn, a product of two major developments:

- a major change in both the nature and intensity of competition
- a substantial improvement in the ability of monetary and fiscal authorities to manage aggregate demand.

The changing nature and intensity of competition has created nothing less than an ongoing revolution in knowledge discovery and invention of which the IT revolution is just a part. It is not a trivial development. It holds the promise of a decades-long duration and a scope that is worldwide. Accompanied by a vast improvement in the ability of monetary and fiscal authorities to manage aggregate demand, the changing nature and intensity of competition will provide long-term support for the two major characteristics of the New Economy:

- rapid productivity growth

1

- low average unemployment coexisting with low average inflation

The productivity growth rate in the United States will average well above the dismal $1\frac{1}{2}$ percent average of the 1970s and 1980s, probably somewhere around the $2\frac{1}{2}$ percent average of the late 1990s. The unemployment rate will likely average somewhat below 5 percent, far less than the average of the 1970s, 1980s, and early 1990s.

The two developments that are creating the New Economy are not accidents of history. They are products of an even more fundamental force—the accumulation of human knowledge together with its practical corollary, the fading away of bad ideas. This report describes the intertwining of the two themes that are so important to the New Economy—the changing nature and intensity of competition and the accumulation of human knowledge. They interact with each other in many ways. Changing competition has created an ongoing revolution in knowledge discovery and invention, but it, in turn, is a product of the fading away of bad ideas.

Chapters 1 through 6 cover the period since World War II and forecast developments a decade or two into the future. The first three chapters describe relationships between competition and the productivity growth rate, the first of the major characteristics of the New Economy. Chapter 4 describes the relationship between competition and the second major New Economy characteristic, low average unemployment coexisting with low average inflation. Importantly, these chapters differentiate between two basic kinds of competition, below-capacity competition and structural competition, and explain how they have interacted throughout the post-war period.

Chapter 7 takes a much longer-term view, describing how the changing nature of competition among *governments* is gradually driving countries away from the warfare that has been the main expression of intergovernmental rivalry in the past. It also explains how competition among governments to attract capital investment is molding the institutions of the twenty-first century in an extraordinarily beneficial manner.

Finally, this report would not be complete without a discussion of stock valuations under New Economy conditions. The stock market bubble of the late 1990s arose from absurd interpretations of the financial implications of the New Economy. Chapter 8 presents an analysis of the valuation of both stocks and bonds based on the expectation of a continuation of New Economy characteristics. We conclude that long-term Treasury obligations were significantly overvalued on a two-to-five-year time horizon with the bellwether ten-year notes at a late 2002 yield of $3^{3/4}$ percent. We also conclude that the S&P 500 stock index was somewhat undervalued on the same time horizon at its late 2002 price of 875. Anyone who is particularly interested in investments should read the last chapter first and then read the whole report from start to finish. Anyone who is especially interested in a nontechnical long-term outlook for the United States and the world should start with Chapter 7.

Chapter 1

THE CHANGING *NATURE* OF COMPETITION AND ITS IMPACT ON PRODUCTIVITY

The fascinating IT revolution of the 1990s, involving mainly computer and communication technology, was but a prelude to the acceleration of knowledge discovery and invention that will occur throughout the twenty-first century. Several powerful forces will drive this acceleration. The first of these forces that we will consider is the changing *nature* of competition in the private production sector. This modification of the nature of competition is forcing, and will continue to force, an increase in the *proportion* of the world's growing human and capital resources that will be devoted to knowledge discovery and invention. It is one of the most important developments in the entire history of knowledge accumulation. It will drive improvements in productivity and living standards.

COMPETITION IS NOW FOCUSED ON THE CREATION OF NEW PRODUCTS

The nature of competition has shifted. In earlier times competition among business firms was mainly in production and selling, using existing technology. Efforts, of course, were made to devise new products and processes, but the resources devoted to such projects were rather modest, and the responsibility for new designs was largely in the hands of people whose main responsibility was production and selling. New developments often came from clever inventors outside the firm or from universities and other organizations financed by government.

As the years went by, firms discovered more and more that the most effective way to compete was to invent new products and processes. They gradually increased their allocation of funds to research and development (R&D). The trend continued until today a significant and growing proportion of the world's resources is devoted to knowledge discovery and invention. This intensifying competition to improve existing products and design new ones accounts for a large part of the ongoing surge in inventiveness.

ESTIMATING CHANGES IN INVENTIVENESS

We could use reported spending for R&D to estimate changes in inventiveness, but unfortunately, statistics for many countries are sporadic and do not go back very far. Therefore, we have turned to the data showing the number of patents granted by the United States Patent Office. Most important inventions made anywhere in the world nowadays result in applications for a patent to the U.S. Patent Office. Consequently, the number of patents granted serves as a rough proxy for the inventiveness of the world.

Chart 1.1 shows the number of patents granted for inventions each year beginning in 1880. Chart 1.2 shows the percentage of total patents that have been granted to foreign individuals, corporations, and governments. Patents granted are not by any means a perfect proxy for R&D spending. The granting of patents lags patent applications, currently by about two years. And patent applications, in turn, lag R&D spending by an unknown period. So there is a double lag between R&D spending and the patents granted figures shown in the chart. Furthermore, all inventions made abroad do not result in patent applications to the U.S. Patent Office. Still, we can make some generalizations about the conditions that encourage inventiveness based on what we see in these two charts.

INVENTIVENESS REQUIRES PEACE AND PROSPERITY

As Chart 1.1 shows, in the mid-1950s the number of patents granted was about the same as the number granted forty years earlier. R&D spending and inventiveness clearly were held back by the wars and the Great Depression. The slump had gone on so long that in the early 1950s a doctoral dissertation and an accompanying article in a professional journal asked whether the rate of invention was declining.[i] But inventiveness soon revived. After World War II, Japan and parts of Europe were in shambles. The recovery of R&D spending and inventiveness was concentrated in the United States where it continued through the 1960s. The decline of inventiveness in the 1970s as shown on the chart was due to the poor economic performance of the United States with its inflation cycle and recessions. During that period R&D spending in Japan and Europe actually accelerated as they recovered from

Chart 1.1 Patents granted, inventions only, U.S. Patent Office

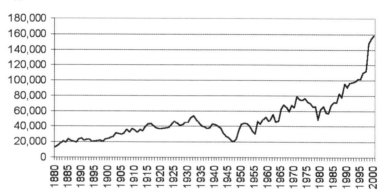

Chart 1.2 Patents granted to foreign individuals, corporations, and governments as a percentage of total, U.S. Patent Office.

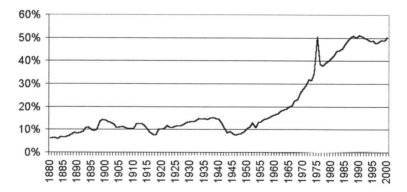

war devastation. Clearly peace and prosperity are basic requirements for R&D spending and inventiveness.

**GEOGRAPHIC SOURCES OF
INCREASED INVENTIVENESS**

Countries can be classified into three categories:

- *Non-modernizers.* In a quite remarkable report entitled *Globalization, Growth, and Poverty,*[ii] the World Bank identified many countries including Pakistan, much of Africa, and countries of the former Soviet Union in which income per head *fell* on average by 1 percent a year during the 1990s. Poverty rose. These countries at the end of the century, in the aggregate, participated less in international trade than they did twenty years earlier. They failed to attract adequate capital investment and did not properly educate their children. They are the nonmodernizers. They have provided little of the world's inventiveness. They are home to about two billion people, about one-third of the world's population.

- *Cheap-labor competitors.* This is the most exciting group of countries because they are going to have such a powerful impact on the world in the twenty-first century. It includes twenty-four countries with a total population of about three billion, almost half of the world's population. These twenty-four countries, identified by the World Bank have in the last twenty years integrated into the world's trading community, moving from the production and export of primary products into manufacturing and even services. The World Bank calls these countries the new globalizers. They rely mainly on cheap labor for their competitive advantage. They obtain most of their technology from advanced countries.

    These twenty-four countries are still very poor, but poverty has declined substantially. During the 1990s, production grew, in aggregate, about 5 percent, more than twice the growth rate of the rich, advanced countries. That 5 percent growth rate is also five times their 1960s growth rate. These countries achieved their new growth status by improving their investment climate to attract capital investment, providing better education, reducing tariffs, and opening up to foreign investment.

Although these countries rely mainly on cheap labor for their competitive advantage, some of them are now devoting more resources to R&D as companies see the necessity for entering the competition to design new products and processes. Nevertheless, only a small part of the world's inventiveness has so far originated in this large group of countries.

• *Inventive competitors*: These countries are the rich, advanced countries and are home to just one billion people, about one-sixth of the world's population. They have provided most of the world's inventiveness because firms in these countries have discovered that the invention of new products and processes is the most effective way to compete. They have devoted large resources to education and have allocated the required capital to R&D to become inventive.

Advanced industrial countries have taken divergent paths toward inventiveness in the past half century. After World War II, the United States took the lead with a burst of R&D spending that resulted in a surge of patents. Part of this spending was financed by government. Japan and Europe lagged behind, but after recovery from war devastation, their inventiveness came on strong. Japan has experienced the largest increase in patents granted to any major country in the past three decades. Growth, however, has subsided in recent years due apparently to Japan's economic troubles.

R&D spending has continued to grow in the major advanced countries, but lately no faster than GDP. In the United Kingdom, Germany, and Italy R&D spending has actually grown somewhat less rapidly than GDP in recent years. Several smaller European countries have increased

R&D spending more rapidly than GDP. They include Finland, Sweden, Denmark, and Ireland.

Most of the countries that now serve as a source of inventiveness had significant industrial bases before World War II. However, there are a few exceptions. South Korea has been an outstanding example. It moved from the nonmodernizer category through the cheap-labor competition stage into inventive competition in half a century. The number of U.S. patents granted to South Korea rose seventy-nine times from 1985 to 1998. In 1998, South Korea spent almost the same percentage of GDP on R&D as did the United States. Almost all countries increase their R&D spending as they industrialize and become prosperous.

INVENTIVENESS IN THE TWENTY-FIRST CENTURY

Current cheap-labor competitors, home to half the world's population, will provide a gigantic burst of inventiveness throughout the twenty-first century. Their governments generally have recognized the need for attracting capital, both foreign and domestic. They are learning, often by making mistakes, how to create the necessary economic and political environment to do so. Some of them have increased their R&D spending, and in a few narrow categories have already entered the inventive competition arena. More patents are flowing to them. As their wage rates rise, their cheap labor advantage diminishes and they are forced to become inventive. The line on Chart 1.2 showing the percentage of U.S. patents granted to foreign individuals and corporations will rise rapidly. How fast it rises will depend on the problem-solving capability of the world's governments. Nevertheless, one should hesitate to bet against the power of the desire to modernize (and the competition to attract capital investment engendered thereby) to dramatically increase the inventiveness, productivity, and living standards of the world.

A child recently born will live to see the number of scientists probing nature's secrets triple or quadruple. And these scientists will be probing those secrets with instruments hardly dreamed of today. A very large percentage of that huge increase in working scientists will arise as the countries we have desig-

9

nated as cheap-labor competitors turn into inventive competitors. Already China alone is graduating far more scientists and engineers each year than is the United States.

The gradual shift of half the world's population from cheap-labor competition to competition in invention will have other favorable consequences beyond speeding the world's technological development. These countries will have to begin looking abroad for sources of cheap labor rather than being a source of cheap labor themselves. They (and present-day inventive competitors) will have to turn to present-day nonmodernizers for cheap labor. This shift has already begun in a meager way. It will smooth the path of those poverty-stricken, stagnant nonmodernizers toward the more rapid growth now enjoyed by the cheap-labor competitors.

Another fascinating implication can be drawn. At the present time hundreds of millions (perhaps billions) of *naturally talented but uneducated* people throughout the world are stuck in jobs requiring little skill. The coming massive shift to competition by invention will require much better education, providing skills to naturally talented people. The proportion of the world's workers with valuable skills will increase and the proportion of workers with few skills will decrease. This shift will improve the bargaining power in the labor markets of less-talented people with few skills, even in present-day advanced countries. Fast-forward a hundred years. Who, in the United States, will do the stoop labor on farms or the dirty work required in cities when there are few immigrants or guest workers coming from cheap-labor-competitive countries? Who will do the repetitive work to manufacture the products now being made in cheap-labor-competitive countries? Much of that labor will be supplied by less-talented people in the United States. Without present-day foreign competition from immigrants and products from cheap-labor countries they will command far better relative pay. The less talented will get a much better deal than they now have.

KNOWLEDGE DISCOVERY AS A CHAIN REACTION

Competition to develop new products is turning knowl-

10

edge discovery into a chain reaction not unlike the one that takes place in an atomic pile. It will have an explosive impact on productivity. Almost all scientists and inventors give partial credit for their discoveries to an idea, discovery, or invention developed by someone else. That is the very essence of knowledge accumulation. Everyone builds upon the past. If new discoveries stimulate other discoveries, and those discoveries stimulate further discoveries, a chain reaction builds. The energy (new discoveries) released by this chain reaction depends on the number of participants involved and the speed of communication among them. As competition to develop new products and processes spreads around the world, the number of participants in the struggle increases. Communication improves daily. A discovery or invention made anywhere in the world is soon made available to, and benefits, the rest of the world. Indeed, the technological underpinnings of productivity and the New Economy could be explosive.

We will probably one day reach limits to the *rate* of technological change in each industry. Obsolescence may come so fast that firms will delay the adoption of a new technology in the expectation that cost effectiveness would warrant waiting for a further improvement. Rising costs of R&D in relation to the commercial value of discoveries may slow development. Only time will tell how soon those limits will be reached in each individual industry. Technological change will, of course, continue to create new industries in which those limits are far distant.

THE IMPACT OF THE IMPROVED ORGANIZATION OF RESEARCH AND DEVELOPMENT

The increasing proportion of the world's resources devoted to knowledge discovery and invention is not the only important development. Improved organization of research and development activities has also had a positive impact.

In earlier times, research and development by corporations was done by individual departments within a firm. However, as R&D became more important, specialized

11

research labs were set up to manage that function. Those labs began appearing early in the twentieth century, but they came into their own only after World War II. They have grown to be extremely efficient operations. They can bring together the efforts of scientists from several disciplines and facilitate the exchange of ideas among them. They can establish working relations with other companies including suppliers and customers. They can build financial and professional bridges to universities, government departments, and private research organizations. They can gain feedback from all the departments in their own company. Perhaps most important, they have the financial clout to delve deeper into the mysteries of nature to pursue long-term goals and thus advance the function of knowledge discovery.

After World War II, part of the research done in universities was financed by government. It was directed mainly toward defense, but included research on weather, energy, and space exploration. However, in the late 1960s, this source of funding began to dry up, and universities turned more to private industry for research projects and funding.[iii] We now have a vast network of private companies, universities, governments, and private research organizations that support one another in knowledge discovery and invention on a worldwide basis.

THE IT REVOLUTION

Considerable effort has been made to compare the IT revolution with technological revolutions of the past such as those ushered in by steam power, railroads, textiles, and automobiles. The objective has been to use the evidence of the impact and durability of past revolutions to predict the ultimate impact and durability of the IT revolution, and correspondingly, the durability of the New Economy. This approach is not likely to be very useful. Previous technological revolutions were revolutions in a particularly important sector of technology as is the IT revolution. The revolution we are concerned with is different. It is a revolution in the whole process of knowledge discovery and invention, includ-

12

ing the amount of resources devoted to the process, the way it is organized, and the competition driving it.

There is no end in sight. Surely parts of the IT revolution, such as the personal computer, will mature to a slow growth rate or even decline, but other aspects of technology will take their place, leading to a long-continued improvement in technology and productivity. And so the new era of large and growing resources devoted to knowledge discovery and invention, driven by competition, will continue to be a major supporting pillar of the New Economy. Although we cannot possibly visualize the end, either in time or in consequence, of this ongoing acceleration of knowledge discovery and invention, we can see in it the promise of an amelioration of some of the problems that distressed the twentieth century and are still with us.

In summary, then, the changing *nature* of competition toward a greater emphasis on the discovery of new ideas, products, and processes would by itself warrant great optimism about the future of the productivity growth rate. But it is augmented by the changing *intensity* of competition, which has in recent years provided another powerful boost to the growth rate that will likely be long lasting. This is the topic we turn to in the next chapter.

Chapter 2

THE CHANGING *INTENSITY* OF COMPETITION AND ITS IMPACT ON PRODUCTIVITY

The intensity of overall competition in the United States (in product, service, labor, and financial markets) is not a constant. It varies appreciably, and the changes must be considered in analyses of inflation, unemployment, and productivity. Over the past half century, overall competition has intensified substantially due to three structural developments: first, a major increase in international trade; second, a substantial improvement in the opportunity for new competitors to enter the arena; and third, an important improvement in antitrust activity coupled with considerable government deregulation. Overall competition has also intensified since 1980 due to a weakening of several transient impediments to competition, described in Chapter 5, that had arisen in the period between 1965 and 1980. The increased intensity of competition since 1980 has slowed the inflation rate and increased the productivity growth rate.

GROWTH OF INTERNATIONAL TRADE

The growth of international trade has sharply increased the intensity of competition in the manufacturing sector of the U.S. economy. Chart 2.1 shows the dollar value of imported manufactured goods as a percentage of the income generated by domestic manufacturing. The increase is startling. We are now importing manufactured goods valued at three-quarters of the income we are generating through production of manufactured goods for both domestic consumption and export. That is up from less than 10 percent a half century ago. In just the last ten years the percentage has risen from less than 50 percent to 75 percent. Almost every sector of the manufacturing industry has felt an increase in competition from imports.

14

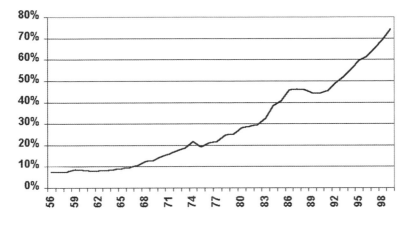

Chart 2.1 Dollar value of manufactured imports as a percentage of domestic manufacturing income. Source: Bureau of Economic Analysis.

Few observers of the business scene would doubt that that increased international competition has restrained inflation and improved productivity. Nevertheless, statistical support can be found in studies by Burton Klein published in 1977, 1984, and 1988.[iv] He found that those industries most impacted by foreign competition had the most subdued price increases. He also argued that those highly impacted industries had the greatest productivity improvements.

The beneficial impact of international trade on competition and productivity is clear. Yet could this present magnificent (but incomplete) structure of international trade, investment, and competition come crashing down as a smaller version did in the early twentieth century? Two major dangers exist: high unemployment and the possible onset of a major war. High unemployment puts tremendous pressure on politicians to try to preserve jobs by reducing imports. A major war would shatter international cooperation with indeterminate consequences. We must leave an appraisal of the severity of these risks to later in this report. But, in summary, we predict that except for brief and infrequent recessions, unemployment will be kept reasonably low, first by the much improved ability of monetary and fiscal authorities to manage aggregate demand, and second by the likely continuation of improved competition built into the structure of the economy. A fascinating change in the nature of competition among *governments* will likely lead to a long-term decline in the incidence of war, as will be discussed in Chapter 7.

On the positive side, powerful forces are driving the world toward economic integration. Perhaps the most fundamental force can be dignified by the title "the Areal Law of Specialization": *the greater the variety of goods produced, the wider the trading area necessary to obtain adequate specialization.* In agricultural-handicraft economies, a trading area of just a few miles was adequate to find specialists for most of the limited items used. Today, the extensive variety of products requires a worldwide trading area to find specialists that can efficiently produce each of those products. The variety of desired and needed products will continue to increase. No country or group of countries will be able to find the specialists for efficient production without *extensive* trade beyond existing borders.

Mistakes will continue to be made. Some impediments to international trade will arise. But no single country can quit the international trade and investment community without seriously jeopardizing its economic prosperity. A tit-for-tat trade war involving several countries always seems to be on the verge of breaking out, but somehow disputes get resolved through the World Trade Organization or otherwise. Such trade disputes will likely be kept within workable bounds since the alternative would be so onerous. A trade war would quickly result in higher unemployment, greater inflation, worsening poverty, and lower productivity growth as international competition declined.

EXPANSION OF THE OPPORTUNITY TO COMPETE

A description of topics such as the impact of international trade on the intensity of competition and the productivity growth rate is useful and should be persuasive. Yet, that description somehow fails to capture the spirit of the frenzied competition and innovation that so enthralled the American public in the 1990s with its young companies and young billionaires. Granted that the enthusiasm was way overdone

16

and has waned with the bursting of the stock market bubble, many of those new companies are, nevertheless, still with us and dominate several parts of the IT industry. Another force, perhaps as fundamental as those we have described, has supercharged competition and innovation. That force is a *vast expansion of the opportunity to compete.* Improved access to investment capital and to education are the two major streams feeding that growing opportunity to compete, bringing a torrent of activity.

Improved access to investment capital has allowed innovative young people to introduce new products without going through long periods climbing the corporate ladder. Also, employees in existing companies who are frustrated by the unwillingness of superiors to undertake promising new projects can leave the firm and find the capital to strike out on their own. The history of IT is replete with interesting stories of revolutionary products that were invented in established companies but were developed and made successful by employees who left the companies, raised the necessary capital, and started ventures on their own.

Venture capital and the NASDAQ "stock exchange" have been the two major sources of capital that have funded this extensive new opportunity to compete. Venture capital has been around for a long time but, as is well known, showed spectacular growth in the past decade prior to the collapse of the stock market bubble. Investment made by venture capitalists starts with seed money, to allow an inventor or scholar to prove a concept. This is the most important capital investment from the standpoint of knowledge discovery and is the riskiest but potentially most profitable aspect of venture capital financing. If the concept is successful, start-up funds are provided to develop products and to begin production and marketing. Several waves of expansion funding are sometimes necessary. Finally, the venture is ready for an initial public offering of stock which can be successful because the relatively new NASDAQ is there waiting to raise enormous sums of money for stock issued by promising companies. The amount of seed money provided by venture capitalists is small in relation to the total amount of investment capital needed for research and development. But it is of enormous importance in providing opportunity for innovative people to enter the competitive fray. [v]

Venture capital has an impact on competition way beyond its initial amount. Large existing companies are often tempted to hold off introducing new products until they have recovered their capital investments in old products. But with the little companies threatening their markets, they have no choice. They must spend on R&D for new products. They must introduce new products before they have recovered their investments in old products. Someone has said that the greatest monopolist profit is a quiet life. With innovative people having the opportunity to compete outside the existing corporate structure, corporate executives seldom get to enjoy the quiet life.

Greater opportunity for education has also added to the opportunity to compete. Financial barriers to higher education have been reduced. Opportunities for women and minorities to obtain better education have increased. Admission to some prestigious universities, whose graduates have often found their way into powerful positions in government and business, is now based more on merit than lineage. Openings to these routes to power are thereby expanded.

And so the opportunity to compete continues to spread as new people have access to investment capital and necessary education. One can only marvel at the impact on competition and productivity this major pillar supporting the New Economy will have as billions of people throughout the world gain the opportunity to compete in the coming century.

IMPROVEMENT OF ANTITRUST ACTIVITY AND DEREGULATION

Among capitalist countries, the United States has taken the lead in protecting competition through antitrust legislation. The United States has also led in deregulating industries that had been subjected to intense government regulation. Deregulation widens the scope of competitive markets in allocating resources, restraining prices, and stimulating productivity.

The impact of antitrust enforcement on competition is considered in an excellent study by W. B. Shephard in which he documented the increase in competition in the United States from 1939 to 1980.[vi] He examined three-digit industries (as classified by the Commerce Department) for the two periods from 1939 to 1958 and from 1958 to 1980. In the earlier period, changes in competition were modest. In the second period, industries generating 20.4 percent of national income moved from the pure monopoly, dominant firm, and tight oligopoly categories to become effectively competitive. This left just 2.5 percent as pure monopoly, 2.8 percent as dominate firm, and 18.0 percent as tight oligopoly. Antitrust enforcement and the threat thereof were the most important factors, accounting for about half the shift to effective competition. Increases in international trade and economic deregulation together accounted for the rest.

As for economic deregulation, several industry-specific studies of deregulated industries have been undertaken. Airlines and trucking were partially deregulated in 1978. Regulation in several financial and communication sectors has since been reduced. In most cases, those actions expanded the effective jurisdiction of competition and increased productivity. Much of this deregulation occurred near or after 1980, the terminal date of Shephard's study.

But there is another extremely important aspect of "deregulation" that should be recognized: *the public attitude toward big business in general.* In the late 1960s and much of the 1970s, a widespread antagonism developed toward big business, especially multinationals. They were accused of raising prices to reap excessive profits, destroying environments, manipulating governments, exploiting minorities, women, and the poor, and engaging in all kinds of vile deeds. But beginning in the late 1970s, and especially in the 1980s, that antibusiness attitude moderated. That moderation was a kind of non-industry-specific deregulation. High marginal tax rates were reduced as part of a widespread tax revolt. Faith in the ability of government to run economic affairs gradually waned as blame for economic problems shifted from business to government. Surely this shift in the public attitude toward business helped improve business confidence, resulting in the sharp rise in business fixed investment that has done so much to restrain inflation and improve productivity. Distrust of business has again arisen. But this time it is more of an attack on corruption and not a broad amorphous accusation against business in general like the distrust that persisted in that earlier period. Recent outbreaks of antibusiness sentiment at the Seattle WTO meeting were more akin to those earlier accusations.

Antitrust legislation and deregulation in the United States can best be appreciated by comparisons with Japan, which opted for a system based largely on intricate cartels cooperating with banks and governments. Japan is now trying, painfully, to reduce those cartel arrangements to make the economy more flexible and competitive. Europe also lagged the United States in protecting competition but has made great strides in supporting competition in the Euro zone.

Multinational corporations now have to run the gauntlet of antitrust enforcement in many countries in which they produce or sell, but for most multinationals the only serious antitrust problems are in the United States and Europe. These barriers to merger can be significant, as demonstrated by the General Electric/Honeywell case where the merger was approved in the United States but denied in Europe. For multinationals antitrust legislation may become more restrictive.

DISCIPLINING BUREAUCRACIES

The three factors described above that have increased the intensity of competition have had a positive impact on bureaucracies and their productivity. *Any large organization not facing the discipline of competition will become stagnant, inefficient, and eventually corrupt.* Why? Because sooner or later managers begin to make decisions more for their own personal benefit than for the benefit of the organization as a whole or for the benefit of the customers they should be serving. Personal security of managers often takes precedence over risk-taking. Change involves risk-taking. So organizations become stagnant and inefficient. The personal interests of managers often expand to outright corruption. The larger the organization, the greater the problem, because managers of individual divisions begin making decisions for their own personal benefit rather than to improve the efficiency of the *organization as a whole* or add to the benefits of customers. Intense competition with other organizations forces managers to make changes and become more efficient to avoid losing their customers or other clients.

Modern technology has decreed that many of us must work together in large organizations. The need to discipline these bureaucracies makes the maintenance of intense competition an absolute necessity. That is why we have begun this report by designating the changing nature and intensity of competition as the central feature of the New Economy.

The bureaucracy problem applies not only to business firms but also to governments, unions, religious organizations, charities, and so on. Competition is difficult to maintain for many of these organizations, particularly governments. Governments must eventually be disciplined by democratic processes that are slow and often ineffective. However, a new competition among governments to attract capital investment is developing. As described in Chapter 7, this new competition will deliver extraordinary benefits to the world in the twenty-first century.

∗∗∗∗∗∗∗∗∗∗∗∗∗∗∗∗∗∗∗∗∗∗∗∗∗∗∗∗∗∗∗

In the first two chapters we have argued that the revolution underlying the New Economy is not just a revolution in IT but rather a revolution in the entire process of knowledge discovery and invention. The changing *nature* of competition and the increased *intensity* of competition have propelled this revolution. These changes have been developing irregularly since the end of World War II. Improved productivity is one of the major benefits of this revolution. Why then did the productivity growth rate begin to decline in 1965, bottom out in 1980, and then take another fifteen years to return approximately to the pre-1965 growth rate?

Three reasons explain that long period of dismal growth in productivity. First, the basic factors involving the changing nature and intensity of competition impacted competition and productivity mainly toward the end of the century. Second, a grievous error by the Federal Reserve initiated the decline in competition and productivity after 1965. And finally, a whole series of structural impediments to competition arose after 1965. Although those impediments began to weaken toward the end of the 1970s, some of them still hampered competition and productivity for several years.

An analysis of the Federal Reserve error and the impediments to competition will be made in Chapter 4, describing the coexistence of low unemployment and low inflation in the New Economy. But first, two special aspects of the competition-productivity relationship should be considered. How does competition affect the productivity growth rate over the business cycle? Here again we take issue with conventional wisdom. And how does competition affect the relationship between the productivity growth rate and inflation, a relationship that has been noted in economic literature but not properly analyzed?

Chapter 3

TWO SPECIAL ASPECTS OF THE COMPETITION-PRODUCTIVITY RELATIONSHIP

Rapidly improving productivity is a major characteristic of the New Economy. Its relationship to the changing intensity of competition is demonstrated by its behavior over the business cycle. In this case the changing intensity of competition involves a special kind of competition—below-capacity competition.

COMPETITION AND PRODUCTIVITY OVER THE BUSINESS CYCLE

Conventional wisdom has it that the productivity growth rate declines as we go into a recession and rises during periods of recovery. But in fact the evidence appears to indicate that the opposite is most often the case.

The bottom line on Chart 3.1 shows the productivity growth rate for nonfinancial corporations. The vertical shaded areas mark the *declining* phase of the business cycle. As the chart shows, the productivity growth rate has begun to *rise* at or near the beginning of each declining phase and has then declined irregularly through each advancing phase — except the last one (more about this later). Why has the productivity growth rate behaved in this manner?

The productivity growth rate rises in the declining phase of the business cycle *because competition becomes more intense* as firms compete more aggressively for shrinking orders and as workers compete more aggressively for limited job openings. The opposite is true in the advancing phase. Surely, few observers of the business scene would argue that the intensity of competition does not strengthen as business activity weakens. But why does that more intense competition improve the productivity growth rate? Simply because firms are forced to improve efficiencies to protect profits and

23

sometimes even to survive. In each business downturn, the newspapers are filled with announcements of cost-cutting measures and restructurings. The evidence in the chart of the rising productivity growth rate in business contractions should not be surprising.

Chart 3.1 Nonfinancial corporate productivity growth rates, five-quarter moving average, and manufacturing capacity utilization, five-quarter moving average. Source: Bureau of Labor Statistics

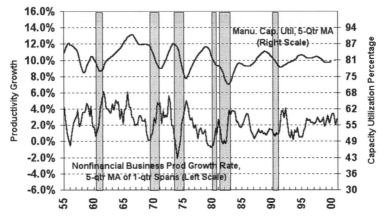

Another extremely useful concept should be introduced at this time. The top line on Chart 3.1 shows capacity utilization for manufacturing. In periods of business contraction, of course, business activity drops further below full-capacity output, thereby intensifying competition. We call this increased competition *below-capacity* competition. It is in contrast with *structural* competition, the intensity of which is determined by factors built into the structure of the economy such as the amount of international trade, labor union density, antitrust legislation, and a host of factors as far afield as the effectiveness of education in preparing young people to compete effectively in the labor market.

Structural competition generally (but not always) changes slowly. But most important, it does not respond, or at least responds slowly, to changing aggregate demand. Therefore, it cannot be changed easily by monetary and fiscal policy. On the other hand, the intensity of below-capacity competition *can* be changed rather quickly by changes in aggregate demand. Consequently, *the intensity of below-capacity competition can be changed by monetary and fiscal policy.* Changing the intensity of below-capacity competition by changing aggregate demand has become the major tool by which the Federal Reserve controls inflation. (More about this in Chapter 4.)

Four other observations can be made about the changing productivity growth rate over the business cycle:

- First, the increased efficiency occurring during business contractions may be due largely to improved *management* or *organizational* productivity rather than to important technological advances. In every business there are difficult, risky, and often unpleasant changes that should be made but are postponed simply because they are difficult, risky, or unpleasant. Such changes may include the closing of failed stores, the abandonment of mistaken policies, or the layoff of poorly performing managers. Declining profits under intensifying competition prod management to action. Economic adversity may also provide a convenient excuse for management to correct mistakes it has not wanted to admit in the face of constant critical observations from stockholders and security analysts.
- Second, in Chart 3.1 we have related the *nonfinancial corporate* productivity growth rate to *manufacturing* capacity utilization. Data are not available for capacity utilization for the entire nonfinancial corporate sector. Nevertheless, it is not unreasonable to assume that the ebb and flow of aggregate demand over the business cycle creates capacity utilization rates for the entire nonfinancial corporate sector quite similar to those of the manufacturing sector.
- Third, the reported productivity growth figures are highly erratic from quarter to quarter, probably due to measurement problems more than changes in the actual rate of growth of productivity. The sawtooth nature of reported quarterly data suggests that errors made in one quarter are overly compensated for in

the following quarter, leading to errors in the opposite direction. This overcompensation leads to still another overcompensation, producing the sawtooth pattern. Various statistical methods for smoothing these numbers show slightly different timing of changes in the productivity growth rate in relation to the beginning and ending of business contractions. We have tried several smoothing devices, and most of them support our thesis of a reasonably reliable positive relationship between the productivity growth rate and changes in the intensity of below-capacity competition. (The four-quarter span published in *Business Cycle Indicators* is not centered, and therefore shows a distorted view of fluctuations relating to the beginning and end of the business cycle.)

- Fourth, the positive productivity growth rate and below-capacity competition relationship does not hold in long contractions such as the Great Depression.

COMPETITION, PRODUCTIVITY, AND INFLATION

The relationship between the productivity growth rate and inflation has been noted in economic literature but not properly analyzed. As Chart 3.2 indicates, the productivity growth rate and the inflation rate have had a rather dependable *inverse* relationship for more than forty years.

Before we examine the causal forces behind this relationship, let's look at the remarkable implications *if the relationship continues to hold*. The Federal Reserve has committed itself to achieving a low *average* inflation rate in the United States. It has not set a precise target, but appears to be aiming at about 2 to 2½ percent a year—a range that spans the targets of most central banks around the world. If the Federal Reserve achieves a low inflation rate, and *if the relationship between the productivity growth rate and inflation holds*, then both lines on the chart will extend far to the right at about a 2½ percent rate. By pegging inflation at a low average rate, the Federal Reserve will also be pegging productivity growth at a relatively high rate. That will double the hourly income and output of the average worker in about thirty years and quadruple it in about sixty years. It will be a far more rapid rate of growth than the 1½ percent average that prevailed for much of the period from 1965 to 1995. That dismal growth rate would have taken nearly fifty years to double the hourly income of the average worker and a hundred years to quadruple it.

Chart 3.2 Changes in the CPI and business productivity growth rate, three-year moving average. Source: Bureau of Labor Statistics.

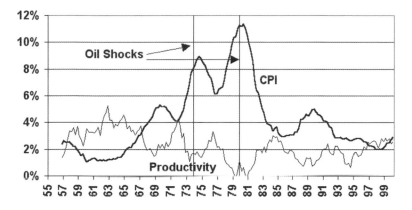

The implications of this possible outcome are so remarkable that we must make every effort to determine what forces produced that long forty year inverse relationship and whether those forces are likely to continue. In the past, economists have used statistical techniques to try to determine if one of the two variables was a dominant factor causing changes in the other. This is a difficult and often inconclusive statistical process, but it produced some evidence that changes in the inflation rate caused opposite changes in the productivity growth rate.

We take a different view. Both the inflation and productivity growth rates were determined by a third factor, *the changing intensity of competition* in the overall economy including product, service, financial, and labor markets. Part of this conclusion comes from a simple observation of the business scene. When competition is intense, business firms attempt to increase or at least protect their profits the only way they can, by improving productivity. When competition is weak, firms attempt to increase or at least protect their profits the easy way by raising prices. Therefore, when competition is intense, inflation is weak and the productivity growth rate is strong. The opposite is true when competition is weak.

The intensity of competition in the overall economy cannot, of course, be measured directly by aggregating the intensity of competition in all its many sectors. Throughout this report we cite enough evidence to be reasonably comfortable with the conclusion that changes in the intensity of competition do have an impact on the productivity growth rate. And few would doubt that changes in the intensity of overall competition have an impact on the inflation rate. Indeed, the changing inflation rate can be considered a useful inverse proxy for the changing intensity of competition since it is the most reliable product of the changing intensity of competition. Many of the "external shocks" that impact the inflation rate, such as the 1970s oil shocks due to the activation of the monopolistic OPEC oil cartel, are really changes in the intensity of competition.

The relationship between the productivity growth rate and the inflation rate becomes clearer when we review the transmission mechanism by which the Federal Reserve controls the inflation rate. It does so by *changing the intensity of below-capacity competition.* Economists may conclude that that statement is a major departure from orthodox monetary theory. It is not. The Federal Reserve controls inflation by tightening money, slowing growth in the stock of money, raising interest rates and changing inflation expectations, thereby slowing growth in aggregate demand. But it is not changes in the money supply, interest rates, inflation expectations, or even aggregate demand that *by themselves* limit inflation. It is the increase in below-capacity competition that occurs as changing aggregate demand moves total output further below existing capacity.

The transmission mechanism by which monetary policy affects inflation has been much debated in economic literature. Sometimes it has been described as a mysterious black box. We suggest that an emphasis on the changing intensity of below-capacity competition provides the most meaningful view of that transmission mechanism. Importantly, the transmission mechanism also changes the productivity growth rate as just described. The Federal Reserve is changing the productivity growth rate as it changes the inflation rate.

Inflation is always and everywhere a monetary phenomenon. That statement, or a variant of it, is probably the most oft-repeated statement in all of monetary literature. In a narrow sense it is correct, but as frequently used, it is misleading or downright wrong. It is correct in the sense that monetary restraint could, and most often should, be used to control inflation. Therefore, when inflation accelerates, it is because of the failure to use monetary restraint, and so inflation is a monetary phenomenon. However, many factors other than an expansion of the monetary aggregates *cause* inflation to accelerate. The sharp decline in the effectiveness of competition in the oil industry due to the activation of the OPEC oil cartel is one such causal factor. Government regulation that forces prices up, overriding the efficacy of competition, is another. Many more such factors could be cited. Therefore, as we look to the cause of inflation we must look to many factors outside the monetary sphere, as most economists now do.

The Federal Reserve can have a powerful impact on below-capacity competition, but it cannot control structural competition quickly. To repeat, structural competition is defined as competition controlled by factors built into the structure of the economy *that do not respond, or respond but slowly*, to changing aggregate demand. The interaction between the changing intensity of *structural* competition and *below-capacity* competition can best be understood in the context of an analysis of the unemployment rate, a topic to which we will now turn.

Chapter 4

COMPETITION AND UNEMPLOYMENT

The first three chapters emphasized the relationship between competition and the productivity growth rate, the first major characteristic of the New Economy. This chapter describes the relationship between competition and the second major characteristic—low average unemployment coexisting with low average inflation.

WHAT DETERMINES THE UNEMPLOYMENT RATE?

The unemployment rate is determined largely by two factors: the intensity of *structural* competition and the capability of the monetary and fiscal authorities to manage aggregate demand. In managing aggregate demand they are managing below-capacity competition and helping to manage unemployment, which is the best single measure of below-capacity competition in the labor market.

When structural competition is sufficiently intense to hold the inflation rate within the acceptable target zone, additional supplementary below-capacity competition is not necessary. But if structural competition is so weak that it allows the inflation rate to rise above that zone, the Federal Reserve must supplement the inadequate structural competition with below-capacity competition by tightening money and thereby slowing growth of aggregate demand. The weaker the structural competition, the more below-capacity competition is required, evidenced by unemployment in the labor market. The high unemployment of the 1970s was due to very weak structural competition requiring considerable below-capacity competition. Chapter 5 will detail the history of structural and below-capacity competition since World War II. As previously described, we believe that several forces have increased the intensity of structural competition enough to allow the Federal Reserve to hold *average* unemployment somewhere between 4 and 5 percent for the coming decade or two.

How Skillfully Can the Federal Reserve Manage Aggregate Demand?

Strong, steady structural competition and low *average* inflation and unemployment rates are enormously valuable attributes. But they are not enough. The monetary authorities (with a little help from the fiscal authorities) need sufficient skill to prevent large fluctuations in aggregate demand that produce alternating periods of inflation and unemployment around the average inflation and unemployment rates. Do they have that skill?

The record of the past two decades is highly encouraging. In twenty years the United States has suffered just two small recessions, and both of them were associated with little wars. Without those wars we might possibly have had twenty years with no recession. Compared with the previous history of the United States, that two-decade period was a magnificent performance. Furthermore, in that period the authorities provided sufficient monetary restraint to maintain below-capacity competition (unemployment in the labor market) at a level high enough to bring the inflation rate down from the 5 percent that prevailed after the initial recovery from the intermittent recession of 1980–82. If that correction of past policy mistakes had not been necessary, the twenty-year performance would have been even better.

What have the monetary authorities learned that made possible their achieving such improved performances? Importantly, they have learned that accelerating inflation must be attacked early before inflation expectations become firmly established. For example, in 1994 some precursors of inflation showed up, and inflation began a mild acceleration. The Federal Reserve, in the face of considerable criticism, tightened money moderately. The growth of business activity and the inflation rate slowed for a few months. Then, business activity began to accelerate, and the United States settled in for five more years of growing business activity and moderating inflation. A similar procedure was followed in 1988–89 and again in 1999–2000 with somewhat less favorable results, partly due to the associated wars. In any event, the practice of attacking inflation early appears to be a rather well-established precedent and should bode well for the future management of aggregate demand.

Inflation expectations, once established, are hard to break, and they tend to perpetuate, or even accelerate, the inflation rate. Much has been written in economic literature about wage norms, the tendency for a pattern of wage changes to persist. The pattern of *accelerating* wage rates in the 1970s was so hard to break that the severe intermittent recession of 1980–82 was required to bring it under control.

One other fact gives assurance that the Federal Reserve will stick to its commitment to maintain a low *average* inflation rate. Federal Reserve authorities know that if they don't, the bond market will do it for them. Any indication that the Federal Reserve is weakening in its resolve raises inflation fears, causing bond prices to drop and interest rates to rise. If carried on for long this trend will reduce aggregate demand, slow the economy, increase below-capacity competition, and bring inflation under control. Why didn't bondholders do that during the 1970s? Because they thought the inflation would be temporary. We know this because they were buying bonds at prices that would provide a satisfactory yield *only if inflation soon slowed dramatically*. Surely we can count on reasonably prompt anti-inflation action in the future. And that is one of the important requirements for the survival of the high productivity growth rate and low unemployment in the New Economy.

SOME BAD IDEAS OF THE PAST ABOUT MANAGING AGGREGATE DEMAND

A brief review of some of the bad ideas that have influenced monetary and fiscal policy in the past helps us to appreciate recent improvement in the management of aggregate demand.

At the onset of the Great Depression the prevailing wisdom was that aggregate demand needed no management. The economy would, by itself, recover from any downturn if left alone. Consequently, other policies took precedence. The perceived need for a balanced federal budget led to a tax *increase*. The perceived need to protect the dollar in foreign exchange markets led to monetary tightening. Both policies added to the decline of aggregate demand and deepened the depression.

Going back still further, an inordinate distrust of centralized money and banking systems was a very bad idea that led to primitive, erratic money and banking systems in the United States for more than a century. Those systems, in turn, produced several money panics and waves of bank failures that intensified (or caused) fluctuations in aggregate demand, producing periods of business depression and slow economic growth. Although the establishment of national banks in 1863 and the Federal Reserve in 1913 helped somewhat, a reasonably effective national monetary and banking system with adequate regulation and deposit insurance did not appear until 1935. Banking reform was triggered by an extreme wave of bank failures that gravely exacerbated the decline in aggregate demand in the early 1930s, helping to produce the high unemployment of the Great Depression. Since the 1935 reforms, bank failures in the United States have been virtually nonexistent. Waves of bank failures no longer weaken aggregate demand. Savings and loan associations required some additional protection in the post–World War II period.

Now fast forward to the late 1960s and the beginning of the great postwar inflation cycle. After more than a decade of stringent fiscal and monetary policy that had brought the postwar inflation under control at the expense of four recessions, the Federal Reserve relaxed anti-inflation monetary policy, allowing a substantial escalation of inflation. The notion (since repudiated) that significantly lower unemployment could be achieved by just a moderately higher inflation rate was apparently an important factor behind this shift in monetary policy. The downgrading of the use of monetary controls in favor of fiscal tools, a doctrine inherited from the 1930's Keynesian revolution, also may have weakened Federal Reserve resolve. The Federal Reserve may have been waiting for the fiscal authorities to take responsibility for inflation control with an anti-inflation tax increase, which finally came but was too little too late. In any event, the permissive monetary policy exacerbated subsequent events, including the oil shocks, leading to an escalation of inflation that finally peaked in 1980 and then took many years to heal.

Still another bad idea inadvertently complicated monetary policy. The Federal Reserve, it was argued, should keep the money supply growing at a constant rate regardless of current events or economic forecasts. This program would be a mechanical management of the money system run by a computer. Steady growth of the money stock was supposed to stabilize the economy. The plan was doomed to fail, for two reasons: First, the relationship between the growth of the money supply and economic activity and inflation *on a short-term basis* is not sufficiently reliable to keep prices and output at satisfactory growth rates. Second, the *technology of money* is constantly changing, making it difficult to know what measure of the money supply to target. New products such as money market accounts at brokerage firms kept appearing, blurring the distinction between money and other assets. The definition of money kept changing, *requiring judgmental changes* in the money supply targets. The changing technology of money made mechanical control of the money supply impossible.

The plan to establish a fixed growth rate for the money supply was never adopted, but it did apparently have some negative impact. The minutes of the meetings of the Federal Reserve Open Market Committee show that the members argued incessantly about which of many available measures of the money supply they should use as a guide. This indecision apparently postponed the adoption of an effective anti-inflation policy. No vigorous sustained action was taken to tame inflation until 1980. Then, under the courageous leadership of the newly appointed Federal Reserve chairman, Paul Volker, severe monetary restraint broke the inflation cycle at the expense of the serious intermittent 1980–82 recession.

CAN THE MANAGEMENT OF AGGREGATE DEMAND BE IMPROVED?

Few would argue that the irrational exuberance that drove the wild speculation in the bull market of the late 1990s did not have a negative impact on the American economy. Among other things, it created excessive spending in some areas that produced later offsetting reductions in spending that helped create the 2001 recession. Should monetary restraint have been used to reduce that excessive speculation?

To have used rigorous and broad monetary restraint to slow the economy just to curb speculation at a time when inflation was not a problem would not likely have been possible or desirable. Even a bit of jawboning by the Federal Reserve raised considerable criticism. However, a tool not used for a generation might have been refurbished for service—raising margin requirements on stock purchases. The Federal Reserve cannot easily justify an attempt to restrain increases in stock prices driven by cash purchases, but it can easily justify the restraint of stock speculation fueled by credit. Speculative buying of stocks on credit has too often in the past resulted in market crashes that have adversely impacted the economy, not to mention inflicting considerable personal pain on many individuals.

The great bull market of the late 1990s was clearly driven by speculation. Stock market credit was a factor. Outstanding credit grew at roughly the same rate as market prices, but they both grew several times faster than GDP. Had margin requirements been raised by several incremental steps, perhaps even to 100 percent, that speculative excess would have been dampened somewhat and considerable pain to the economy and to many individual investors would have been avoided. Stock market credit is only a small part, under 2 percent, of total stock market valuation, *but it was a much larger part of the stock speculation that exaggerated the bubble frenzy.*

An unfenced swimming pool in which children could accidentally drown is a danger considered by law to be an "attractive nuisance," and the owner can be prosecuted. A rising speculative stock market is also an attractive nuisance. It usually proves irresistible to millions of uninformed people (especially in its later, most dangerous stages) who watch their friends make easy money and who listen to respected financial analysts tout new purchases on TV programs. The Federal Reserve should be certain that such stock speculation is not fueled by the dangerous use of credit.

How Dangerous Is
A Worldwide Deficiency of Demand?

Controlling *excessive* demand and inflation has been a primary concern of the United States and much of the world since World War II. In 2002 the specter suddenly arose of a possible worldwide multiyear period of deficient demand with its accoutrements of slow economic growth and excessive unemployment. How dangerous is this problem? Japan, the United States, and the Euro zone raise the greatest concern since they consume the lion's share of the world's industrial output.

Japan has suffered more than a decade of economic stagnation due in large part to inadequate demand. Japan has simply not had the political capability to solve the problem. Inadequate demand has been due to the collapse of almost unbelievable real estate and stock market bubbles, which burst suddenly in 1990 but have continued to deflate ever since. Home prices have declined for eleven years. The negative wealth effect and the fear of further declines in asset prices have cut back the Japanese willingness to spend. The decline in the value of collateral behind loans produced a plethora of bad debts and left the banking system in shambles. The result: inadequate demand.

Many changes should be made in Japan to stimulate spending, but the failed banking system is at the heart of the problem. No country can do well without an efficient financial system to channel funds from savers to spenders and to create new money as needed to maintain adequate demand. Japan's political system has so far not been up to the task. However, as Japan lags behind its competitors, pressures will build on its political system, forcing the necessary changes. That time may not be far away.

Could the United States duplicate the Japanese experience? As in Japan, a large stock market bubble has burst. But the American bubble was almost trivial compared to the Japanese twin stock market and real estate bubbles. Furthermore, the U.S. banking system is still in excellent shape. Nevertheless, the United States has faced a triple threat. The stock market bubble produced excessive spending by corporations and individuals. The reaction to that excessive spending produced lower than usual spending. The events following the September 11 tragedy further weakened confidence and spending. Finally, the corporate scandals raised many doubts about the accuracy of reported earnings and the safety of investments, intensifying stock market losses. In the face of these three negative events, efforts to stimulate spending have so far been reasonably effective. Sharp declines in interest rates together with tax cuts and tax rebates have encouraged spending and kept the recession shallow. If these efforts are insufficient to bring complete recovery from the 2001 recession, more aggressive fiscal policy in the form of tax rebates and increased spending will be required. And that poses a problem—a fear of government deficits.

In the half century of fighting inflation after World War II, government deficits quite properly gained a bad reputation for aggravating inflation and crowding out private investment, thus slowing growth. These adverse effects of deficits do not exist in recession; nevertheless, the fear of government deficits is widespread, and that fear may inhibit the necessary use of expansionary fiscal policy if monetary stimulation is not adequate and slow growth persists. Yet this danger is probably moderate in the United States, and further fiscal stimulation will likely be used if necessary. Political squabbling as to the form the stimulus should take will likely delay its application. The risk is high of a slow year or two recovery from the 2001 recession.

As for the Euro zone, the fear of deficits promoted the adoption of the stability and growth pact which was designed to limit deficit spending. This pact may already be inhibiting fiscal stimulation thereby casting a shadow over the likelihood of prompt recovery to acceptable growth in Europe. Of course, slowness in improving structural competition, especially in labor markets, is an even greater worry.

With slow growth in Japan, the United States, Europe, and South America, the world faces a significant test of its ability to stimulate aggregate demand. A failure due to fear of deficits at a time when inflation is not a problem and when growth is slow would be unfortunate.

Using Fiscal Policy to
Increase Aggregate Demand

The Federal Reserve has demonstrated its ability to control inflation. Also, it has several times succeeded in accelerating business activity by the easy-money stimulation of aggregate demand. But what can be done if the United States faces a time when monetary tools have been *fully exhausted*, the economy remains depressed, and inflation is not a problem—a situation such as Japan has faced? Political pressures are such that we will certainly turn to fiscal stimulus. Will we use it wisely or badly?

Forecasting the amount of stimulus needed to produce adequate growth is extremely difficult. That simple fact dictates the requirements of a program to use fiscal policy to increase aggregate demand.

- The program must be flexible—quick to start and easy to stop when fiscal stimulus is no longer necessary. Also, it needs the ability to make midcourse corrections.
- The program should not involve overhauling the tax code or initiating long-term spending programs. Bad long-term law, hastily designed, can too easily be passed under the pressure to provide quick, short-term stimulation. Long-term tax and spending bills should pass or fail on their own merits, not because a short-term stimulus to the economy is needed.
- Contingency plans should be set up in advance to facilitate a quick start.

The following is one plan that meets the above requirements. Congress could authorize the President to mail out checks every three months in the amount of, say $100 to $500 to anyone who had paid social security taxes anytime in the previous two years. Most of the unemployed would receive checks. Money would come from general funds not from the social security trust funds. The Secretary of the Treasury would maintain constant consultation with the Federal

Reserve and with the President's economic advisers to determine when fiscal stimulus is needed and the amount of the quarterly payment.

If Congress insists on making each quarterly decision as to the need for, and the amount of, the stimulating payment, mechanisms would have to be devised to avoid committee delays and to keep extraneous matters from being considered.

This plan would give the President (or the Congress) a flexibility in stimulating the economy almost equal to that of the Federal Reserve in controlling inflation. The fear of government deficits should not prevent the enactment of such a plan. In time of recession deficits do not crowd out private investment. Deficits at such time are financed by *new money* created by the banking system, thereby holding interest rates down. Also deficits do not accelerate inflation unless aggregate demand becomes excessive. The flexibility of the plan allows for a speedy end to stimulation should such a situation arise.

The plan has built-in controls against abuse. Over-stimulation that threatened inflation would call forth a rebuke by the Federal Reserve in the form of tight money with unpopular rising interest rates. The President (or Congress) would also be anxious to end the program to preserve funds for *permanent* spending and tax-cutting proposals.

We view a program of this nature as essential insurance against an extended period of below-trend growth and high unemployment. But it would also have other virtues. It would likely make future recessions even shorter and milder than the little ones we have experienced in the last twenty years. It would also relieve the Federal Reserve of the necessity of making highly aggressive interest rate cuts such as those made in 2002. Extremely low short-term rates work a hardship on the millions of people who rely on interest from savings accounts and other short-term investments, slowing their spending in the process. Furthermore, the ability of extremely low short-term interest rates to significantly stimulate aggregate demand is highly problematic. Unusually wide swings in interest rates add an element of instability to the economy.

The government (including the Federal Reserve) must manage aggregate demand. Improved management accounts for much of the improvement in economic performance over the last century. Providing short-term fiscal stimulation in recessions is the main gap yet to be filled. This plan is one option for providing that support. A flexible plan of this sort should be implemented immediately.

The problem of stimulating an economy with high unemployment *and also with an inflation problem* requires an improvement in structural competition, a topic that we have described earlier, and to which we will return now and at other times in this report.

How Low Can Unemployment Go

How low can we drive unemployment without causing inflation to accelerate? Economists call this point the "non-accelerating-inflation rate of unemployment", or NAIRU. For a long time in the 1970s, 1980s, and early 1990s, that point was believed by many economists to be fixed at 6 percent. Since unemployment hovered below 6 percent for several years after 1995 without triggering inflation, the NAIRU came to be regarded as variable, and various statistical devices were developed in an attempt to estimate a likely range of variation. We have argued that the lowest point to which unemployment can be driven without accelerating inflation is determined by the changing intensity of *structural* competition and is likely to average somewhere around 4 to $4^{1}/_{2}$ percent for the next several years. Unwise policies that throw up impediments to structural competition (described below under policy requirements) could, of course, upset this forecast.

Unemployment Around the World

Virtually every government in the world, at one time or another, faces the difficult problem of improving the availability of jobs for its citizens. Sometimes this problem is just sporadic. Frequently, it is continuous. The problem shows up as unemployment, underemployment, and the lack of interesting jobs that can lead to better pay and personal satisfaction.

As indicated earlier, a country requires two effective

forces to maintain low unemployment: adequate aggregate demand and intense structural competition. The spending of money (demand in the marketplace) initiates economic activity. It actuates the placing of orders, the hiring of workers, and the paying out of income. It keeps the wheels of commerce turning. Structural competition, on the other hand, is the controller that channels demand into increased production rather than into increased prices that would require an application of greater below-capacity competition (unemployment in the labor market). Countries with high unemployment are deficient in one or both of these two forces.

Keeping demand adequate has generally (but not always) been the easier of the two forces to maintain. It is usually done by holding interest rates low, increasing government spending, or cutting taxes, all of which governments like to do. *Excessive* demand, producing inflation, has more often been a problem in the past half century than *inadequate* demand.

As for structural competition, the gross deficiencies are so well known they hardly require description. They show up as unwise government regulation, protected monopolies, limits to international trade, powerful labor unions, corruption, inadequate education, inefficient capital markets, and many other weaknesses. Nonmodernizing and cheap-labor-competitive countries are especially negligent, but even advanced inventive competitors have deficiencies. The recent high unemployment in parts of Europe, for example, is frequently blamed on rigidities and unwise regulation in the labor market.

How can deficiencies in structural competition be repaired? Responsibility for improving competitive markets rests with individual governments. Fortunately, successful countries are serving as instructive examples and putting pressure on laggard governments to undertake change. The twenty-four cheap-labor competitors, making up half the world's population, have made some changes and are reaping the benefit of those changes. Each has serious problems yet to be solved, but competitive pressures to solve them are so great and the prizes so enticing that it is highly unlikely that these countries will abandon the struggle for modernization for long.

One conclusion seems clear. *Many (probably most) governments have within their grasp adequate tools to significantly reduce unemployment.* In a few countries, structural competition is sufficiently intense (and other conditions are in place) to allow the government to boost aggregate demand simply by more aggressive monetary and/or fiscal policy without accelerating inflation. Most countries, unfortunately, require the more difficult policy of improving *structural* competition so that inflation does not accelerate when more aggressive monetary and/or fiscal policy is applied.

China may be an example of the first category. It has no significant inflation, no foreign exchange problem, no foreign debt, huge cash reserves, an enormous supply of underutilized labor, and a large unmet need for infrastructure. For the past few years China has been expanding government spending through deficit financing to stimulate the economy, to meet pressing infrastructure needs, and to put more of its unemployed to work. Some critics have begun to warn of excessive use of deficit financing, but as yet inflationary signs of excessive demand have not appeared. Perhaps monetary and fiscal policy may be able to speed China's already rapid growth rate even more.

As for reducing unemployment by improving structural competition, the Netherlands has been a kind of poster child example of sharply reduced unemployment achieved by reining in the wage-boosting power of monopolistic labor unions and by improving government regulation of labor markets. *The Economist* describes the Netherlands approach: "Here, what was once one of the highest jobless rates in the EU has become the lowest (barely 2%)—and without vast pay differentials or the abolition of the welfare state. Instead, in the early 1980s the trade unions agreed to restrain wage demands. In return firms created more jobs and the government reduced social-security contributions. The government has also reduced jobless benefits, tightened eligibility for claimants, and lifted restrictions on part-time work."[vii]

Other high-unemployment countries have far more difficult problems: Argentina has a high foreign debt denominated in foreign currency that restricts policy options. Germany and France have powerful, less cooperative labor unions. India has a fractured political system that cannot adequately undo decades of policies dedicated to small-scale production and national economic self-sufficiency, nor can it mitigate the inherited problem of religious strife. Many non-modernizing countries have even greater problems. No one can expect the creation of an efficient competitive market to be quick or easy. Nevertheless, unemployment around the world will slowly recede as impediments to structural competition are reduced.

Policies That Keep Unemployment Low Will Also Keep the Productivity Growth Rate High

In this chapter we have described the necessity for maintaining adequate aggregate demand and intense structural competition to keep unemployment low. Those policies will also keep the productivity growth rate high.

In 2002 Jason G. Cummins of the Federal Reserve Board and Giovanni L. Violante of University College, London, published a fascinating study on the "technology gap." This gap shows how much more productive the best available machines are than the average machine in use. The findings of the study are impressive. In the 1950s the productivity of the best available equipment was about 8 percent greater than the average equipment in use. By the early 1990s the gap had widened to about 37 percent. In the late 1990s it widened a bit further to about 40 percent in spite of a massive capital spending boom. How accurate are these estimates? Measurement problems are extreme, but the conclusions are roughly supported by surveys of executives who indicated that they had put to use only a fraction of the best available new equipment. What important conclusions can we draw from this study?

The study clearly shows that there are two aspects to the problem of improving productivity by technological change. First, the world's inventiveness must create new technology, and second, firms must be induced to adopt that new technology. In part, however, the gap is just a normal lag. Greater inventiveness as shown by increases in patents granted (see

Chapter 1) generally results in a wider gap. Faster development of new products requires a longer time to be accepted. But that is not the only factor involved. What conditions might induce businesses to increase investment in new equipment utilizing the large existing backlog of technology that can increase productivity?

Certainly the necessary stimulus for new investment in plant and equipment is no mystery. The expectation of future prosperity with rising demand and reasonable profit margins is most important. These are precisely the conditions created by the policies that keep unemployment low—maintenance of growing aggregate demand and intense structural competition. If business activity remains sluggish in 2003 there will be no excuse for governmental failure to use aggressive short-term fiscal stimulus to spur business activity. Such stimulation would quickly move the economy toward full employment and toward utilization of the huge backlog of productivity-enhancing technology currently available.

In Chapter 1 we described powerful competitive forces that have been driving the inventiveness of the world. These forces will cause inventiveness to accelerate in the new century. Nevertheless, even these powerful forces can be temporarily interrupted by recession and slow growth. Both inventiveness and the adoption of new technology are hampered by economic weakness.

How does this argument, that prosperity is essential for productivity improvement, square with the observation made in Chapter 3 that the productivity growth rate actually accelerates in the contraction phase of recessions? Improved productivity in recessions is due mainly to improvements in management productivity rather that improvements in technology. But if an economic downturn continues for long, the low spending for plant and equipment will soon slow the productivity growth rate as it did in the Great Depression.

Better management of aggregate demand and more intense structural competition have been the major factors behind improved economic performance over the past century. The use of fiscal stimulus by a flexible plan similar to the one recommended in this chapter can further improve eco-

nomic performance when monetary stimulus has been largely
exhausted and inflation is low.

Chapter 5

THE HISTORY OF STRUCTURAL AND BELOW-CAPACITY COMPETITION SINCE WORLD WAR II

This chapter describes the interaction of changes in structural and below-capacity competition since World War II and shows how those changes produced the depressing record of the inflation cycle. It also describes the events that culminated in the New Economy, finally blossoming in the 1990s.

From World War II to 1965: Taming Inflation

The United States exited World War II with a burst of inflation created by excessive aggregate demand due to wartime shortages of consumer goods and high consumer liquidity stemming from large accumulated savings. Until 1965, inflation control was high on the agenda of monetary and fiscal authorities cooperating to restrain aggregate demand. Four recessions (1948-49, 1953-54, 1957-58, and 1960) were the penalties paid for the restraint on growth in aggregate demand. The resulting below-capacity competition was evidenced in the labor market by unemployment rising to between 5 and 7 percent in each recession. The unemployment rate showed a gentle upward trend from the end of the Korean War to 1961.

By 1961, low inflation expectations (wage norms in the labor market) were well established. As a reward for taming inflation, monetary authorities were able to allow faster growth for five years and still maintain low inflation and low unemployment. Worker compensation (wages plus benefits) grew quite steadily at around 4 percent a year, and consumer prices generally increased a little less than 2 percent a year. The unemployment rate gradually declined to nearly 4 percent. Productivity grew rapidly. The intensity of structural competition held quite steady over that five-year period.

Perhaps stable wage norms were the most important part of the stable structural competition. Wage norms generally respond but slowly to changing aggregate demand and are therefore, by definition, part of structural competition. The excellent economic performance of the first half of the 1960s had been earned by the disciplined management of aggregate demand and below-capacity competition in the 1950s. Then came the tragic error that launched the United States into an inflation binge that didn't peak until 1980 and took many years thereafter to heal.

BELOW-CAPACITY COMPETITION
OVER THE INFLATION CYCLE, 1965-95

Chart 3.2, page 27, should serve as a guide to the changing inflation rate and productivity growth rate produced by the changing intensity of overall competition during the thirty-year period from 1965 to 1995.

During this period, the first blow to the effectiveness of competition in performing its functions of restraining inflation and spurring productivity growth was delivered by the Federal Reserve. In 1966, and for the following three years as the inflation rate accelerated, the Federal Reserve retreated from its responsibility to restrain inflation, a responsibility it had so carefully nurtured for the previous fifteen years. It allowed demand to grow so rapidly that output pushed up against capacity, eliminating necessary below-capacity competition. *Necessary* below-capacity competition is the amount of slack that allows markets to function effectively. In the labor market, unemployment (a measure of below-capacity competition) dropped below 4 percent in late 1965 and stayed there for four years. In the product market, industrial production rose to 90 percent of capacity, and in the important residential shelter market, rental vacancy rates dropped to the 5-to-6-percent range from the $7\frac{1}{2}$-to-$8\frac{1}{2}$-percent range where they had stayed for several years. These three developments were important examples of output pressing strongly against capacity, thereby largely eliminating below-capacity competition. Thus, a period of excessive inflation and low productivity growth with all their

47

unfortunate accoutrements was launched, not to be brought under control for more than a quarter of a century.

During the 1970s, the Federal Reserve twice made half-hearted attempts to bring inflation under control by monetary restraint. In 1970, and again in 1973–74, demand was curtailed, slowing output and increasing below-capacity competition, bringing about the two moderate recessions of those years. But several impediments to *structural* competition had developed so much that moderate applications of below-capacity competition could not bring inflation down or restore a vigorous productivity growth rate. Finally in 1980, Paul Volker, the newly appointed chairman of the Federal Reserve Board, aggressively tightened money, thereby reducing demand and dramatically increasing below-capacity competition. It was necessary shock therapy. Unemployment rose to nearly 11 percent and industrial capacity utilization dropped below 70 percent. The inflation rate, of course, quickly declined. The economy embarked on a healing trend. Since then, substantial strengthening of structural competition supplemented by reasonably moderate and judicial use of below-capacity competition has brought the inflation rate and productivity growth rate back close to the levels of the early 1960s.

STRUCTURAL COMPETITION
OVER THE INFLATION CYCLE, 1965-95

During the entire period from 1965 to 1995, the forces changing the nature and intensity of structural competition described near the beginning of this report were slowly gathering strength. Unfortunately, several impediments to structural competition arose beginning in the last half of the 1960s. They overwhelmed those nascent forces that were strengthening competition. In fact, they were so strong that even the moderate applications of below-capacity competition in the two recessions of the 1970s were inadequate to tame inflation. Not until the drastic application of below-capacity competition in the 1980-82 intermittent recession was the back of the inflation cycle broken. Six of those impediments to structural competition will be briefly considered.

1. *Energy costs.* The most dramatic events affecting structural competition were the oil shocks of late 1973 and 1979 indicated by the two vertical lines on Chart 3.2. The first oil shock occurred about eight years after inflation began to accelerate in 1966 and the second shortly before inflation peaked in 1980. We cannot blame the long inflation episode on the oil shocks. They exacerbated the problem by sharply reducing competition in a major industry, but they did not create it. Several other factors weakened *structural* competition beginning long before the first oil shock. These factors, *in total*, probably weakened structural competition about as much as or more than the activation of monopoly power by OPEC in the oil industry.

The inflation rate tripled from 1965 to just before the first oil shock in late 1973, indicating a substantial decline in the intensity of overall competition. Nevertheless, below-capacity competition (as measured by the capacity utilization rate in manufacturing and the unemployment rate in the labor market) had actually strengthened by the time of the first oil shock. This implies that *structural* competition (the other part of overall competition) had already weakened substantially by the time the first oil shock struck. What were those other structural factors that weakened overall competition?

2. *The costs of a third-party-payment health-care system.* In the past half century, the United States has shifted from a reasonably competitive, private fee-for-service health-care system to a third-party-payment system in which the third parties are government and employer-financed insurance. This change has moved a significant amount of decision making away from the discipline of competitive markets, thereby reducing structural competition and increasing health-care costs dramatically. When medical bills are paid by a third party, patients have little incentive to limit the quantity of services demanded or to search out the lowest-cost providers. Providers, in turn, often have little incentive to limit either the quantity of service provided or the prices charged. More often their personal incomes depend on increasing the quantity of service provided at higher charges.

The big surge in third-party payments came in the late 1960s with the establishment of Medicare and Medicaid, probably stimulating the rapid growth in private, employer-financed health insurance that had begun during World War II. Since the increased health-care costs affected most employers in much the same way, and since they often came as a surprise, these costs were likely shifted to the consumer in higher prices rather than being shifted back to workers in the form of slower-growing wages. The net result was a sharp increase in medical costs as a percentage of GDP and an intensification of inflation. Personal health-care expenditures rose from about 5 percent of GDP in 1966 to nearly 8 percent in 1980. We estimate that in the 1970s the *direct* impact of the third-party-payment health-care system on inflation amounted to a quarter of the impact of the oil shocks, and it began much sooner. Therefore, the *indirect* impact was greater since inflationary forces had much more time to work through the price-wage-price spiral. (Estimates of the impact on inflation of health-care costs and all other factors are extremely crude. Adequate data are simply not available for rigorous analysis.)

As we shall see, most of the impediments that weakened structural competition during the period of accelerating infla-tion up to the late 1970s soon reversed course. But the third-party-payment system was an exception. It continued to boost health-care costs as a percentage of GDP until about 1993. The burden of rising health-care costs spawned two counterdevelopments designed to limit those costs: expanded government regulation to limit price and quantities provided, and managed health-care systems such as HMOs. The capi-tation payment system of HMOs reduced the pressure on providers to expand the quantity of services provided, but in trying to hold those services down they irritated patients who did not feel compelled to reduce their demands for services that for them were nearly free. Medical costs as a percentage of GDP held steady for four or five years after 1993. But those costs have now begun to accelerate again as managed health-care systems have come under increased criticism and are forced to expand their services. How the resolution of the conflict between third-party payers trying to limit costs and patients demanding more "free" services is resolved will be important in determining the effectiveness of structural competition in controlling the health-care inflation rate in the years to come.

3. *The union wage premium.* Several studies have documented a sharp rise in the union wage premium in the early 1970s. This overriding of competition by unions in the labor markets was not due to any new legislation, but was rather an activation of the latent power that unions had received from the 1935 National Labor Relations Act and the vast increase in union membership during, and immediately following, World War II. The limits to that union market power had not been tested in the 1950s and early 1960s.

The rise of union wage premiums had a profound impact on inflation in the 1970s, and it began at least three years prior to the first oil shock. Yet those high premiums did not last. They began to decline in the late 1970s, and together with the decline in union membership, reduced the union impediment to structural competition. For most of the 1990s, union wages (including benefits) grew less rapidly than nonunion wages, indicating a weakening of union bargaining power. A great deal of this weakening was due to increased international competition, which held down prices, making large wage increases impossible.

We estimate that the *direct* cost of the rising union wage premium had about one-fourth the impact on inflation in the 1970s that the oil shocks during that period did. Since the inflationary impact of the rising union wage premium came sooner, the *indirect* impact through the wage-price-wage spiral was proportionately larger than the *direct* impact.

4. *Residential shelter costs.* Residential shelter costs account for 29 percent of the CPI and therefore should get special attention in an analysis of inflation rates. Vacancy rates are a measure of the relation of output of residential shelter service to the capacity for producing such service at any one time. The higher the vacancy rates, the more slack there is in the market and the greater the rent-restraining competition. Ordinarily, vacancy rates are counted as repre-

senting *below-capacity* competition since those vacancy rates can be influenced moderately by changes in monetary policy. Interest rates certainly affect housing supply, and doubling up of household units in recession affects demand. Yet, sometimes supply and demand for housing get so far out of balance that shifts in monetary policy cannot easily rectify that imbalance. As Chart 5.1 shows, such an imbalance existed in the United States from about 1967 to about 1983. We therefore count the low vacancy rates during that period as representing mainly weak *structural* competition.

Chart 5.1 Vacancy rates. Source: Bureau of Economic Analysis

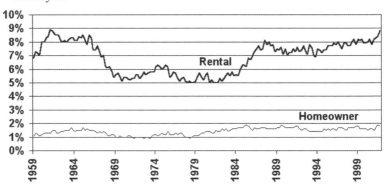

The failure of new construction to respond adequately to the demand for housing during that period was likely due substantially to uncertainty as to how long the inflation would last, together with the high cost of mortgage funds that prevailed in the inflationary environment. If a builder signed up for a high-rate mortgage loan and then inflation and interest rates soon declined, he would be at a serious disadvantage in competing with newly constructed low-interest-rate financed homes. The federal rent controls from 1971 to 1973 and subsequent rent controls in a number of local urban jurisdictions may also have had an impact. In any event, the inflation-disciplining force of structural competition in the housing market during that period was limited as compared to both the prior and subsequent periods.

We estimate that rising shelter costs in the late 1960s and 1970s had only about one-eighth the *direct* impact of the oil shocks on inflation. Yet, they began several years sooner and therefore had a large impact on inflation though the indirect route of the price-wage-price spiral. We should also note that the impact on inflation would have been somewhat less had the present method of computing homeowners' equivalent rent been used at the time.

As the chart shows, vacancy rates (and structural competition in the shelter market) rose sharply beginning in the early 1980s and have remained high. The high vacancy rates in rental housing may have accounted for the relatively slow growth of rental costs in the early 1990s. However, rental costs have recently begun to accelerate along with the market price of homes.

5. *Social regulation.* The compliance costs of social regulation grew rapidly with the establishment of the War on Poverty and Great Society programs of the late 1960s. Environmental legislation was the single most important part of this social legislation from the standpoint of the impact on compliance costs. Social regulation moved a great many cost decisions from the jurisdiction of competitive markets to the jurisdiction of government and generally drove those costs higher. Therefore, the efficacy of structural competition was reduced.

To quantify this weakening of structural competition is extremely difficult because of the lack of data. The best single study is the oft-quoted one by Thomas D. Hopkins, "The Cost of Federal Regulation."[viii] But this study covered only a short period of time and relied solely on cost estimates made by government regulators, who have a strong incentive to underestimate the cost burden of complying with regulation just as the regulated industries have an incentive to overestimate those compliance costs. Nevertheless, we believe those compliance costs may have had as much as one-sixth the *direct* impact on inflation that the oil shocks had in the 1970s. The *indirect* impact was probably somewhat greater as they began much earlier.

6. *Reservation wages.* A reservation wage is a wage below which workers will choose to remain unemployed rather than

work for less than that wage. A reservation wage can be changed substantially by changing the amount of unemployment insurance and/or welfare benefits to which the unemployed worker is entitled.

During the late 1960s and part of the 1970s, both unemployment insurance and welfare benefits became substantially more attractive, giving workers an incentive to remain unemployed. For example, the percentage of the labor force covered by unemployment insurance rose from about 70 percent in 1965 to more than 85 percent in 1979, after which it leveled off. The length of time a worker could receive unemployment benefits also expanded. Studies have shown that lengthening the time during which unemployed workers can receive unemployment compensation increases reservation wages and contributes to longer unemployment spells.

The vast expansion of welfare programs in the late 1960s is well known. They bear the titles of Aid to Families with Dependent Children, food stamps, Medicaid, and Supplemental Security Income. These programs resulted in a doubling of welfare expenditures from the mid-1960s to the mid-1970s. Welfare rolls grew substantially even during the periods of rapid business expansion and low unemployment when they would normally be expected to decline.

We have not as yet attempted to estimate how much the liberalization of unemployment insurance and welfare benefits kept workers off the market and thus reduced competition in the labor sector, but it likely resulted in a significant increase in the unemployment rate in the 1970s. Welfare programs were cut back substantially in 1996, and news reports indicate substantial increases in enrollments in job training programs and reduction in welfare rolls. It is, of course, still too early to judge the success of these welfare reforms, but so far they have apparently added workers to the competitive labor market.

An Overall View of the 1965-95 Inflation Cycle

What important overall observations can we make about the complex interactions of below-capacity competition and various kinds of structural competition over the thirty-year inflation cycle?

First, as previously explained, the oil shocks were not the predominant cause of inflation. The *initiating* cause was the tragic failure of the Federal Reserve to provide sufficient below-capacity competition to bring the accelerating inflation under control in the four years beginning in 1966. The Federal Reserve error was accompanied by and followed by several kinds of weakening structural competition, of which the oil shocks were but one.

Adding up the estimates of *direct* impacts of the changes in five non-oil elements of structural competition indicates that they had nearly the same direct impact on inflation as did the two oil shocks. Furthermore, most of them preceded the first oil shock by a few years and thus had a longer time to impact inflation *indirectly* by working through the price-wage-price spiral.

Second, all of the factors that affected structural competition were products of government actions. The oil shocks were imposed by the foreign governments that controlled OPEC. The others were products of internal U.S. legislation. And all this legislation that weakened structural competition was a product of the belief that a market economy requires government intervention to provide a safety net for the unfortunate, to equalize incomes, and to protect the environment. Related thereto was a conviction on the part of many that big business (especially multinational corporations) was behaving badly and needed to be punished.

Clearly, Medicare and Medicaid, extensions of welfare benefits, protection of the environment, unemployment insurance, rent controls, and other aspects of the War on Poverty and the Great Society were products of the notion that the U.S. market economy required a good deal of government intervention on the grounds of social justice. All but one of the competition-inhibiting factors listed above were products of legislation enacted during the inflation cycle. Only the increased union wage premium grew out of earlier legislation, the 1935 National Labor Relations Act.

Intense competition, with its propensity for creative destruction that causes serious dislocations, will for decades be an essential aspect of a well-functioning economy. Under these conditions it is inconceivable that the American public will abandon the view that government is obligated to intervene in many ways to further a deeply felt sense of social justice. Much of America's success (as well as that of every country) will in the future be determined by the ability to achieve that goal of social justice without harming the structural competition that makes possible low unemployment without inflation (more about this later).

THE NEW ECONOMY, 1995-99

Three major features of the five-year period from 1995 to 1999 combined to convince many that some fundamental phenomena had altered the American economy for the better, turning it into a New Economy. Low unemployment coexistent with low inflation, something that had not happened in America for thirty years, was obvious to everyone. For economists, the remarkable feature was the high productivity growth rate, far above that of any five-year period since the early 1960s. The initially reported, spectacular productivity growth rates have since been revised sharply downward, but they are still impressive. Also, the long period of prosperity in the 1990s without a recession, and the near twenty-year period with just the mild 1990–91 recession, led many to believe that recessions were a thing of the past.

A debate began, yet to be resolved, as to how permanent these New Economy characteristics would be. We have argued in this report that something fundamental has happened to alter the economy. The changing *nature* of competition and three major developments that increased the *intensity* of competition are built into the structure of our economy and will likely be long lasting. Together with a vastly improved ability of monetary and fiscal authorities to manage aggregate demand, they account for a good deal of the New Economy performance. Yet, some less permanent features also helped create those late 1990s economic characteristics.

First, the weakening of the impediments to structural competition described above that had arisen in the 1965–80 period may not be permanent. Those impediments may rise again. As argued in the following chapter, the pressure of very real social problems in the years to come may produce economic solutions that will impede the effectiveness of structural competition, as happened to some extent in the late 1960s and 1970s. And, of course, the OPEC oil monopoly may become much more virulent.

Second, the stock market bubble was certainly of a temporary nature. It helped create the outstanding performance of the late 1990s. That bubble, concentrated especially in Internet companies, was a powerful force. It induced excessive capital investment that was partly wasted. Nevertheless, part of it contributed to the most unusual experience of a rapid productivity growth rate continuing late into a period of economic advance. That had rarely happened before. The stock-market-induced investment also helped to contain inflation by keeping capacity growing ahead of output, thus maintaining significant below-capacity competition late into an economic advance, a feature that was also unusual. Stock market profits made possible rapid growth in consumer spending and large government surpluses. On the negative side, the excess production capacity has to be worked off before recovery in capital investment can once again become vibrant.

No one can demonstrate precisely what proportion of the New Economy characteristics is permanent and what proportion is temporary. Yet, the clear evidence of a substantially improved competitive environment should provide grounds for believing that a significant part of the New Economy characteristics will long endure.

Another overall approach to the events of the late 1990s helps to understand the development of the New Economy characteristics. Turn back to Chart 3.2, page 27. In the absence of a direct measure of overall competition, we have used changes in the CPI as an inverse measure of the changing intensity of competition. It is the most dependable product of overall competition. It has, since 1980, shown a pronounced downward trend indicating an intensification of overall competition. Below-capacity competition actually weakened during this period, so structural competition, the other part of overall

57

competition, must have strengthened substantially. That more intense overall competition, culminating in the late 1990s, produced the upward trend in the productivity growth rate. The strong structural competition reduced the need for Federal Reserve applications of below-capacity competition to curb inflation. Therefore, unemployment was low. Management of aggregate demand by the Federal Reserve was sufficiently skillful to keep a long-term inflation cycle from developing as happened in the late 1960s. Thus the main characteristics of the New Economy fell into place.

We must now ask what policy changes, if any, are required to preserve the New Economy characteristics of low unemployment and rapid productivity growth.

Chapter 6

NEW ECONOMY POLICY
REQUIREMENTS
FOR THE UNITED STATES

Fortunately, no grand new policies are necessary in the United States to preserve the New Economy characteristics of rapid productivity growth and low average unemployment. The changing nature of competition, moving toward greater emphasis on R&D competition, the growth of international trade and investment, a continued enforcement of antitrust legislation, a continued availability of entrepreneurial capital and education that improves the opportunity for new players to enter the competitive arena, and a rigorous anti-inflation monetary policy—these are all trends that are firmly established with great momentum that will not easily be diverted. By themselves, they may be enough to assure a reasonable continuation of New Economy characteristics.

But unfortunately, there is a wide area of social policy encompassing the safety net, inequality in the distribution of income, and the environment that *could*, if badly handled, throw up impediments to structural competition, seriously diminishing the valuable New Economy characteristics. Solutions to these issues of social policy must be found in the face of four powerful trends that will likely persist over the next few decades: rapidly growing wealth, the widening spread between people of great talent and those of limited talent, the growing complexity of human society, and the aging of the population. How will these four trends affect the ever-present social policy debate?

1. *Rapidly growing wealth.* As indicated earlier, the forces that have created the New Economy will likely yield a productivity growth rate somewhere in the neighborhood of $2\frac{1}{2}$ percent. That annual increase would double the hourly output and income of the average worker in about thirty years, and quadruple it in sixty years. With the American economy

generating that kind of wealth, it will likely appear obscene to most Americans not to take reasonably aggressive actions against preventable human suffering. There is little chance that the funding devoted to solving social problems will diminish. It will almost certainly increase.

2. *The widening spread between highly talented and less talented people, particularly as to intelligence.* In general, smart people tend to marry smart people and dull people tend to marry dull people. This will inevitably lead toward a widening of the distribution of mental capabilities. This same process might also occur with other human attributes such as appearance, health, and energy. The New Economy will continue to be a meritocracy. Competition will be paramount. A less intelligent, less attractive, less healthy person will have about as much chance competing against an intelligent, handsome, healthy person as a crippled goat competing with a Bengal tiger. Consequently, incomes will be wildly disparate. Pressure will build for more government spending programs and a sympathetic tax structure.

3. *The growing complexity of human society.* As technology advances, a wider variety of tasks will require a wider variety of specialists. A wider variety of jobs will become available, many requiring highly specialized education and training, making the selection of a trade or profession more difficult. In addition, more jobs will become obsolete, making retraining more important. A wider variety of products will become available, often requiring technical competence to make purchase choices. Saving and retirement plans, including investments and insurance, have become more complicated. Partial privatization of social security would add more complexities. Taxes are rarely ever simplified. How will this growing complexity of human society interact with the widening range of human talents?

4. *The aging of the population.* As the population ages, a growing proportion will become unproductive and less self-sufficient requiring additional support from government or other organizations.

One conclusion is inescapable. Since the proportion of most advanced countries' resources devoted to the solution of social problems is already high and will likely increase, the countries that can find solutions to these problems with the least damage to the incentives and the competition that are required in the New Economy will outperform the others on the world economic stage. Those governments that deny they have any responsibility for solving these problems will fail as badly as those governments that adopt policies they believe will solve the problems but that destroy the incentives and the competition that are essential to the proper functioning of the New Economy.

An illustrative example: The abysmal education system in many of our inner cities is one of the more appalling problems left over from the Old Economy. One solution, offered by the existing education establishment, is to spend more money, retaining the same educational structure. These expenditures would, of course, increase taxes, boosting costs and adding somewhat to the pressure on the Federal Reserve to tighten money, slowing the economy and increasing unemployment.

A voucher system adding competition to the education system is a frequently proposed alternate solution. Parents would have a broad choice of sending their children to public, private, charter, or parochial schools. Consumer choice means producer competition. Competition would have a remarkable impact on education. In Milwaukee, where a meager choice system has been in operation for a few years, an improvement of the public school system has probably been the greatest benefit.

But improvement in the schools themselves would not be the only benefit. A choice system of education would bring an important improvement in education awareness to the community as a whole. Giving parents choices also gives them responsibility. Parents would have to learn more about available schools. They would have to follow their children's performance, watching homework, truancy, and learning progress. They would have to talk to their neighbors about different schools, curricula, and discipline. For years (decades?) the education establishment has urged parents to get more involved with the schools. The best way to do this is to give parents choices and the responsibility that goes with making choices.

Inner city children generally want the voucher system. Their parents generally want the voucher system. All that is missing is political leadership, too much of which is being wasted trying to establish the system in whole states rather than just the inner cities where it is wanted and sorely needed.

THE CRUCIAL DECISIONS AHEAD

And so the basic policy requirements are simple: to maintain those forces described above that have led to the new and more intense competition, and to avoid throwing up impediments to the proper working of that competition. But some impediments may creep in. If they do, the United States will experience a serious weakening of structural competition. That will be the real crunch time. We will face a situation where unemployment is considered to be unacceptably high, and yet inflation is at its highest acceptable level. What will we decide to do? Some will say once again that the Federal Reserve should relax monetary restraint to reduce unemployment through faster growth, accepting a little higher inflation. Others will say that we should hold inflation steady by monetary restraint and accept the high "natural rate" of unemployment. Still others will call for government regulation of wages and prices in critical areas. And some will be heard to say that all we need to do is cut taxes to stimulate investment. Yet, the future of the New Economy will depend on our taking a different course. We must focus our attention on the long, difficult, painful path of improving structural competition.

Chapter 7

THE LONG-TERM OUTLOOK
FOR THE NEW ECONOMY

The very long-term outlook for the New Economy is positively brilliant when compared to the Old Economy encompassing the twentieth century with its wars, depressions, inflations, and grinding poverty around much of the world. And once again, changing competition will be the driving force. In this context, however, the new competition will not be just among private companies but increasingly among governments as well. Competition will also intensify among religions, labor unions, universities, the arts, nongovernmental organizations of all kinds, and ideas in every conceivable category. The New Economy is essentially a global economy. Competition is developing on a global scale.

FORCES THAT WILL MOLD
THE TWENTY-FIRST CENTURY

We shall leave to others the ambitious task of trying to find a single factor that guides the course of human events for all time, whether it be the class struggle, economics (as in an economic interpretation of history), or whatever. But we shall describe the forces that will likely determine the general direction of history through just the twenty-first century. For many centuries the course of human events was directed on a short-term basis largely by the whims, personal preferences, or religious inclinations of individual heads of authoritarian governments—kings, dictators, commissars, chancellors, ayatollahs, and others. But that has changed. In the tiny speck of time we call the twenty-first century, the course of history will, more and more, be determined by *competition among governments to attract capital investment*. Forces that will drive that competition have already been set in motion by existing bodies of accumulated knowledge. How did it happen?

The envy factor. Most of the people living in developing countries, containing 80 percent of the world's population, envy the people living in advanced countries. They envy the dazzling array of consumer goods, the substantial measure of freedom enjoyed, and the interesting jobs available to qualified workers. Great pressure is put on governments to emulate the success of advanced countries.

How can governments of developing countries modernize to copy the success of the advanced countries? They must obtain vast amounts of capital investment together with the necessary technology and management expertise. But capital investment is in limited supply. Each government must compete with other governments to attract that capital. The winners are those who can provide the most attractive environment for investors. This competition to provide the best investment environment will largely mold the institutions of the twenty-first century. Governments in countries we have called "cheap-labor competitors" containing half the world's population have entered the competition with varying degrees of enthusiasm, but all with some degree of success.

How did the advanced countries create the successful political-economic systems that induce such envy and the copying activity that is now under way? These systems are largely the product of three large bodies of accumulated knowledge:

- *Technology*: The vast body of technical knowledge is an obvious source of the New Economy's abundance. It is what the world sees and what the world wants. But by itself it is not enough.
- *Competitive markets*: The discovery that the self-serving nature and the often-described "struggle for status" of human beings can be harnessed by the discipline of competitive markets to serve a very large cooperative community involving billions of people has been a spectacular achievement. It is one of the greatest discoveries of all time. In this community, each worker provides a tiny bit of specialized effort and takes out a tiny bit of the total community output. A large body of knowledge has grown up around

these markets. It includes ways to maintain adequate demand, to protect competition, and to design a money system, as well as solutions to a thousand other problems that arise in competitive markets. This body of knowledge is not yet fully appreciated by many governments. But sooner or later its general precepts will be learned and to a large extent copied. They must be learned to enable a country to attract the capital investment required to gain necessary technology.

- *Democratic governance*: Governments, of course, are absolutely necessary. Without them, all would be chaos. They must set and enforce the rules that allow a market economy to work. To keep governmental powers from becoming the playthings of heads of state, a host of techniques have been developed to enable the citizenry to limit those powers. Improving these techniques is still a work in progress. Democratic controls of government are an important part of our body of accumulated knowledge. They will follow, accompany, or lead the extension of market competition around the world.

These three bodies of knowledge have created the abundance, freedoms, and opportunities now envied by so many who don't have them. They have, therefore, set in motion the competition to replicate that abundance, freedom, and opportunity. In doing so, they have determined the general outline of human development in the twenty-first century.

This report began with the assertion that the world has embarked on an accelerating trend of knowledge discovery and invention. It is ending with the assertion that three bodies of accumulated knowledge have already set the major course of human development for the twenty-first century. Knowledge really is power.

How Competition Will Affect Twenty-First-Century Institutions

One can hardly imagine more favorable circumstances for

the design of twenty-first-century institutions than the intense competition to attract capital investment. Most of the things governments must do to win out in the never-ending struggle to modernize are well known. They include at least five categories.

- Governments must provide a workable, generally accepted rule of law (including an independent judiciary) to protect private property and the primacy of contract. This is essential to attract necessary capital investment from abroad but is also important for attracting capital investment from within a country. Hernando DeSoto of Peru has written a fascinating book, *The Mystery of Capital*, in which he describes how enormous amounts of capital investment could be created by improving the law governing property rights in several poor developing countries. Many farmers, proprietors of small businesses, and home occupants control property only by dint of possession. Property is not officially recognized by deed or other instruments providing legal protection. Therefore, this property cannot easily be used for collateral on which to borrow funds for expansion, including the creation of new capital. It cannot easily be sold to gain funds for capital investment in other ventures. DeSoto calls these assets dead capital that could be activated by giving them the documented legal status already provided to property owned by large enterprises.
- An environment of peace and tolerance is needed to allow buyers and sellers, investors and entrepreneurs, teachers and students to move safely and comfortably around the country, and indeed around the world. Tourism especially requires tolerance, and tourism has become a major source of funds that developing countries can use to acquire capital equipment. Not surprisingly, intolerant Iran has languished near the bottom of the list of countries ranked by foreign tourist income as a percentage of GDP.
- Governments must maintain considerable fiscal responsibility, avoiding unnecessary spending, taxation, and

borrowing. Appropriate bank regulation is an important part of this fiscal responsibility. Failure in the fiscal arena shows up as inflation, lost incentives, excessive budget deficits, widening current account deficits, bank failures, and eventually unemployment and stagnation. Bond, stock, and currency markets nowadays levy severe penalties on governments for lax fiscal policies, discouraging capital investment in the process.

- Besides providing an appropriate legal and fiscal framework, a government must provide a decent human environment in order to attract the best capital investment. Of course, citizens must be properly educated and trained. This is especially true when a country graduates from its initial comparative advantage of providing cheap labor and moves into the competition for designing, selling, and maintaining sophisticated products.

- Corruption must be minimized. Transparency International, a nongovernmental organization, conducts periodic surveys to estimate the prevalence of corruption in various countries. Clearly, the most corrupt countries attract the least direct foreign investment. Corruption is most prevalent when government regulation is extensive, providing an army of regulators with the power to extract bribes in return for favorable decisions. Ration coupons, housing permits, travel authorizations, business licenses, job opportunities—these are examples of the authorizations that government employees can trade for bribes in countries where governments maintain extensive control of an economy. Minimizing corruption generally requires a shrinking of government regulation of economic activity.

Industrialized countries, as well as developing countries, are faced with this competition to attract (or at least retain) capital investment. The competitive pressure to improve the investment climate never ends. Governments of industrialized countries are under pressure to continue making all those improvements that developing countries must make to attract capital investment. When they fail to do so, they see their own firms channel investments to friendlier environments, and they attract little offsetting investment from abroad.

Competition among governments to attract capital investment, of course, has limitations. Obviously, it will not *necessarily* solve problems where solutions require international agreements among competing countries, and where solutions *initially* appear to harm some countries. Global warming may turn out to be a case in point. Yet, international cooperation among competing governments has already racked up some notable achievements. The development of institutions to facilitate international trade is a magnificent accomplishment. International police cooperation is another. There will likely be many more.

Of course, no country has to make all those above-listed reforms before it can begin to attract capital investment. But some progress must be made and a trend toward an investment-friendly environment must be evident. Sooner or later, an investment-friendly government will arise in all countries, as the pressure to modernize becomes irresistible. Countries simply cannot go far toward modernization without becoming part of the international investment community. Unfortunately, in a number of countries, such a government will arise later rather than sooner. Nevertheless, movement toward reform is unmistakable.

Saudi Arabia momentarily appears to be one of a few countries able to become prosperous without following many of the rules necessary to attract capital investment. Its immense oil resources gave it power to flout many rules and still attract capital investment to the oil industry. But even that wealth will not last forever. The problem of attracting capital investment will return. Already the growing population is beginning to put pressure on the government to modernize its policies.

Although we argue strongly that the responsibility for the economic improvement of developing countries lies mainly with those countries, nothing in this report should be construed to imply that that development could not be moderately speeded by intelligent foreign aid from advanced countries or by greater opening of advanced-country markets.

The Coming Proliferation of Meaningful Choice

The strong predictions we have made about the twenty-first century sound highly deterministic as though people have no choice as to what will happen. That's far from the truth. We are simply arguing that the great majority of the world's population has *already* chosen modernization, and that that choice will determine much of twenty-first-century development. The remaining choices involve how to get there, and in these choices people will have considerable latitude. Yet, coming choice will surely be constrained by the need to attract capital and the need to educate populations, both of which will require the policies previously outlined.

Furthermore, people will gain far greater power than they have ever had before to choose where they work, what goods and services they consume, and what kind of government they live under. Through their demand in the marketplace, they will order producers to provide the goods they want. Through democratic processes, they will have considerable power (constrained by preferences of other voters) to control the government policies under which they live. Indeed, the choice of modernization will eventually deliver an enormous range of meaningful choice to people *because* government policy will be constrained by the requirements to attract capital investment and provide adequate educational opportunities.

Impediments to Modernization

The pressures to modernize to achieve the freedoms, the attractive job opportunities, and the wealth of market-managed economies are powerful, but so also are the many well-known impediments. Those impediments include many authoritarian governments, entrenched bureaucrats, monopolists in both labor and product markets, and others who are *initially* hurt by a turn to a competitive economy. Impediments of a social nature include ideas, habits, customs, religious convictions, and embedded hatreds that are difficult to dislodge. But many countries are overcoming these obstacles and are building the investment-friendly environments necessary to modernize. They

69

are setting performance standards by which other governments are judged. The necessity to attract capital will intrude upon many decisions each government makes. Decisions will often be painful. Governments will have to compromise cherished traditions and temporarily alienate some of their people. The pressure to do so will be great.

Myriad forces are constantly interacting with one another to determine the events of the day and to change (or prevent the change of) institutions that will direct the events of the future. Some of these forces are strong. Others are weak. The strong forces are *controlling* forces. The weak forces are *adaptive* forces. When adaptive forces come up against a controlling force, they must give way to that stronger power. We have projected that the need to modernize, working mainly through competition to attract capital investment, will be by far the strongest of the controlling forces throughout most of the twenty-first century. It will be so powerful that it will eventually override those impediments that now seem so intractable but in the end will prove to be just weak adaptive forces. It will overcome opposing ideas and customs, as well as embedded hatreds. It will even force a damping down of such stubborn conflicts as the passion-laden India-Pakistan entanglement in Kashmir and the Israeli-Arab hostilities in the Middle East.

There is no *realistic* alternative to modernization by attracting capital investment. The alternatives so far chosen by some governments (or by the people they are trying to govern) would, if continued, keep their countries in poverty, intermittent military conflict, and hopelessness while they watch a large and growing share of the world move rapidly onto the road toward modernization with its wealth, freedoms, and opportunities. Those alternatives to modernization by attracting capital investment are not realistic. They will eventually be abandoned. If the forces driving modernization are so powerful, does the nature of existing governments really matter? Of course it does. The wisdom, or lack of wisdom, of present-day leaders will determine how long and how painful the transition to New Economy conditions will be.

Many present-day nonmodernizing countries are caught in

a Malthusian trap. Rapidly growing populations are pressing against relatively fixed production capabilities. Standards of living are declining. The only way to break out of this trap is to enter the competition to attract capital investment. To do that countries must move toward those features necessary to attract capital investment described earlier in this chapter. That will not be easy. Countries such as Iran whose leadership is staunchly resisting significant change are inviting an eventual sudden change in leadership. If delayed for long, such change could be violent.

Although impediments to modernization often seem unyielding, we are entitled to look beyond the prevalence of entrenched hatreds and misconceptions, beyond the prevalence of unscrupulous and self-serving governments, and focus on the many places in the world where competition among private producers and competition among governments are making great progress.

BY-PRODUCTS OF COMPETITION
TO ATTRACT CAPITAL INVESTMENT

By-products of the competition to attract capital investment are substantial. Billions of people will move from farms to factories, stores, and offices in urban environments. Their fertility rates will decline, bringing the world's population growth rate down to zero probably not long after the middle of the twenty-first century. Pressure on the world's space will moderate. Funds (and incentives) to protect the environment will become available as modernization brings a moderate degree of affluence.

Our forecast that the output of most developing countries will match the output of advanced countries, which will, in turn, continue to grow rapidly, will give many environmentalists nightmares. Actually, it is the best outcome that environmentalists can reasonably hope for because it is the quickest (only?) way to bring population growth under control. The possibility that developing countries will delay industrialization until their populations have doubled and *then* industrialize should make for far worse nightmares. Rapid

71

industrialization is important.

From Malthus to the present, forecasts of imminent disaster due to limitations of resources have been upset by improving technology. If our analysis in Chapter 1 is correct that the world has embarked on an accelerating rate of knowledge discovery and invention, improving technology should solve problems due to population growth during the period while it is still expanding.

More effective democracy will be another by-product of the competition among governments to attract capital investment. Democracy is not a *prerequisite* for the establishment of competitive markets. In fact, one might argue that the many dislocations, lost privileges, and unequal opportunities that arise in the change from a government-managed economy to an economy managed by competitive markets can best be handled initially by an authoritarian government as long as that government is seriously dedicated to reform.

Though not a prerequisite, substantial democracy will be a by-product of the establishment of competitive markets. A turn away from extensive government management always results in a shrinkage of the power and presence of government. When citizens no longer face government factotums who have great discretion to say yes or no, at the school, store, housing authority, license bureau, ration agency, employment office, and other places, their fear of government diminishes, and they begin demanding more civil and political liberties. The ability of government to track and discipline people wanes. Democratic procedures eventually follow.

Finally, how will competition to attract capital affect the distribution of the world's rapidly growing wealth and income, both among countries and among individuals? The favorable impact of the New Economy globalization of investment, trade, and competition on the equalization of wealth and income is so misunderstood by many who oppose globalization that we must review our analysis made earlier in this report.

The output of present-day cheap-labor-competitive countries containing half the world's population has been growing much faster percentage wise than advanced countries. As their wage rates rise, they will have to turn toward the present-day poverty-stricken, nonmodernizing countries for cheap labor. That will gradually bring those countries into the group that is gaining on the advanced countries. The gap between rich and poor countries will be dramatically narrowed during the twenty-first century.

As for income distribution among individuals, right now there are billions of poorly paid, unskilled (or lightly skilled) workers in the world. They include less talented people and many naturally talented people who never had the opportunity to get the education and training required to command better-paying jobs, even if such jobs were available. But cheap-labor-competitive countries are being forced by competition to provide better education and training and will gradually attract the capital investment that will provide better jobs. Therefore, as the twenty-first century develops, there will be far fewer unskilled workers competing for the same jobs. The less talented will still be doing the drudge work both on farms and in cities, but they will command much better relative pay.

THE CHANGING NATURE OF COMPETITION AMONG GOVERNMENTS

Few will deny that a vicious competition among governments has prevailed during most of recorded history. Much of the rivalry was driven by the desire to achieve wealth, power, and prestige for the governments themselves and for the countries they ruled. Often, the desired power was to extend religious domination. The acquisition of land and its natural resources, together with the people who worked the land, was the primary method of adding to wealth, power, and prestige. But the supply of land is relatively fixed. To add to territorial holdings meant seizing land from some other government. And that usually meant war, the main expression of intergovernmental competition throughout most of recorded history.

Rivalry among governments still prevails and is still being driven largely by the desire to achieve wealth, power, and prestige, too often for the government itself rather than for the country it rules. The big difference is that the technique

73

for achieving those goals has changed dramatically. Whereas the control of land and the people working the land was once the measure of success, nowadays the quantity and quality of productive capital is becoming the critical measure. Adding to *land* meant taking it from another government, usually resulting in war. Adding to *productive capital* more often results in cooperation of governments through international trade and through the functioning of the international investment community, even though considerable bickering arises at the many points where competitors meet. Surely the ability of governments to satisfy the drive for wealth, power, and prestige without resort to war is one of the most valuable gifts of modern technology. As more governments become aware of the necessity to make their countries attractive places for capital investment to achieve those long-standing goals, the New Economy should provide a more peaceful era in which to live.

THE PROBLEM-SOLVING CAPABILITY
OF THE NEW ECONOMY

Might some presently unforeseen event arise that will seriously delay the worldwide extension of the New Economy? Of course it might. And thousands of pundits are constantly predicting dire events if we don't adopt their recommended policies. This is good. Complacency and overconfidence are enemies of any government. As Herbert Muller frequently pointed out in his multivolume series on the history of freedom, "Nothing fails like success." Complacency and overconfidence born of initial success have destroyed countless governments, countries, and empires. Furthermore, the freedom that accompanies (or follows) the development of competitive market economies will allow the release of many bottled-up hatreds and desires that have been suppressed for decades by Old Economy authoritarian governments. Some of those outbursts will be violent. In the transition to the New Economy, the world may seem somewhat more chaotic than before.

If some currently unexpected problem comes along equivalent in seriousness to the twentieth century's Great Depression, will the New Economy be able to solve it? Or will competitive capitalism suffer another long setback like the twentieth century swing to socialism, which was in large part due to the perceived failure of capitalism produced by the Great Depression?

What determines problem-solving capability? *The existence of a large number of capable participants with an opportunity to innovate and under competitive pressure to do so provides the best environment for problem solving.* As competitive market economies spread around the world, these conditions will expand in the private production sector, guaranteeing a widening flow of new, better, and less expensive products and services to solve long-standing problems such as human disease, as well as to satisfy wants that the New Economy will generate. But the more exciting prospect is the new competition among governments.

When the Great Depression struck, there was just a handful of reasonably well-established capitalist countries. Furthermore, most of the economists in those countries had learned their economics out of the same textbooks. Consequently, few innovative approaches to solving the problem were devised until the Depression had done great damage. But now there are many reasonably well established capitalist countries, each one trying to find a superior solution to current problems. We have moved a long way toward the environment of having many reasonably capable government participants with opportunities to innovate and under competitive pressure to do so. Every act of governance now must face critical comparison to its counterparts designed by competing governments in many other jurisdictions. The more successful ones are eventually copied. The chances of solving the problems generated by the New Economy are improving as the number of capitalist governments increases, each trying to outperform the others. For example, look at the variety of approaches to dealing with fluctuating foreign exchange rates. They have varied from free-floating rates to fixed rates buttressed by currency boards that might make the survivability of fixed rates possible. Recent experience appears to indicate that relatively free-floating rates are better, except perhaps in very special circumstances. History has demonstrated that fixed exchange rates without the discipline of a device such as a currency board are disastrous. They have largely been abandoned. This type of experimentation among competing governments will be the wave of the future. It should vastly improve the problem-solving capability of New Economy governments.

OPTIMISM BASED ON GOVERNMENTS' PROBLEM-SOLVING CAPABILITIES

No forecast of the economic and political outlook for the United States and the world more optimistic than the ones we have made in this report is anywhere likely to be found. What do we see that pessimistic forecasters do not see? *We have greater confidence in the ability of governments to solve problems.* Furthermore, we suggest that the accuracy of medium- and long-term forecasts will depend largely on the forecaster's ability to judge governments' problem-solving capabilities.

For example, we expect a return to near full employment in the United States within two or three years from the bottom of the 2001 recession. But some pessimistic economists are projecting a multiyear period of slow growth—under 2 percent. Implicit in that forecast is an increase in the unemployment rate to more than 10 percent. Also implicit in the forecast is a prediction that monetary and fiscal authorities will be unwilling or unable to stimulate aggregate demand sufficiently to bring the unemployment rate down to a more satisfactory rate of, say, 5 percent. We agree that conditions spawned by the bubble years *might* suppress aggregate demand for an extended period. But that is not the question. The question is whether the monetary and fiscal authorities can and will use easy money, tax rebates, tax cuts, and increased spending (all tools that governments love to use) to adequately stimulate demand. We believe they can and will.

As this report has pointed out, a great deal has changed since the inflationary, high-unemployment days of the 1970s. At that time monetary and fiscal stimulation resulted in higher prices rather than higher output and lower unemployment. Structural competition was not adequate to channel increased demand into increased output rather than into increased prices. But as we described in earlier chapters, the intensity of structural competition has improved. The monetary and fiscal authorities will be able to stimulate demand without accelerating inflation if such stimulation becomes necessary.

That is just one tiny example of what we believe is undue pessimism as to governments' problem-solving capabilities. We must now elaborate on our statement that the best conditions for problem solving exist when *many participants have the freedom to innovate and are under competitive pressure to do so.* All three of the conditions in that statement are relevant to government problem solving today—freedom to innovate, a large number of participants involved, and action driven by competition.

- *Freedom to innovate.* For most of the half century since World War II the problem-solving ability of many governments was under the constraint of the Cold War and the socialist dogma that required extensive government management of economic activity. But those constraints were shattered just a little more than a decade ago with the fall of the Berlin Wall leading to the collapse of the Soviet Union. The disclosure of the abysmal performance of the Soviet economy—that paragon of socialism—dealt a near-fatal blow to the already wilting socialist dogma that had shackled policy making in many countries for decades. The end of the Cold War also freed many governments whose policies had been chained to the requirements of the particular Cold War camp to which they were tied. A new sense of freedom to try innovative approaches appeared. A new sense of dynamism arose. The world is now changing at a faster pace, bringing new problems related to the transition to new policies. Governments have far greater opportunity (and pressure) to innovate than they had under the socialist dogma and the Cold War. We wonder how many people fully appreciate the significance to government of this recent outbreak of freedom, innovation, and change.

- *Many participants.* Far more governments are now involved in designing market-managed economies than ever before. The majority of governments have accepted the need to modernize and have recognized (often tentatively) the need to make some change toward a market-managed economy. Each government faces its own particular set of circumstances and problems, so each government has to design a slightly (or vastly) different approach to development. Innovation is essential. Yet, with so many countries involved, each government has examples, some good, some bad, in each stage of development to look to for suggestions. There are now many varieties of free-market economies. There will be more. They arise as many participants experiment with new approaches to solving problems.

- *Competitive pressure to perform.* Governments face serious rivalries in their race to gain wealth, power, and prestige. As described earlier, intergovernmental rivalry nowadays plays out more in the economic and social spheres than in the military sphere as it once did when wealth, power, and prestige were usually gained by taking territory from some other government. But that rivalry among governments is still very real and, we believe, will force governments to take painful steps to solve their problems. For example, how long will proud Germany tolerate being stuck with the accusation that it is dragging down the Euro zone before taking steps to free up its labor market and to make the other adjustments necessary to get its economy moving again? Japan has experienced a decade mired in stagnation and indecision. Yet, poverty has not yet become serious. Unemployment has only recently risen significantly. Japan's loss has so far been primarily a loss of self-confidence and prestige. Its hidebound political system has not yet faced up to the necessity of cleaning up its banking system and making other changes necessary to accelerate growth. We suggest that even Japan's sclerotic political system will soon respond to pressure to keep ahead of its neighbors. South Korea and China are gaining fast. Competition among governments is real. Its power to force governments to solve their problems should not be underestimated. Competition to attract capital investment will put unrelenting pressure on government to perform.

Still another development adds to our optimism about governments' problem-solving activity. *Financial markets have become automatic disciplinarians*, deterring some bad government decisions and encouraging some good ones. Just the talk in official circles of excessive government spending or excessive tax cuts that *threaten to accelerate inflation* will send bond and stock markets down. And that, in turn, threatens recession and the tenure of politicians who face elections. That is, indeed, a powerful deterrent. The Federal Reserve is also under discipline. Today, when it fails to restrain inflation, the bond market declines, thereby increasing interest rates, slowing the economy, and weakening inflationary pressure. As explained in Chapter 5, if the prospect of inflation had impacted the financial markets in the late 1960s as it does today, much of the distress of the long inflation cycle could have been avoided. Of course, the financial markets have useful disciplinary impact on only a fairly narrow range of government decisions. But those decisions are important in the economic sphere.

Finally, we come to the last of our reasons for improved optimism—the fading away of bad ideas as described in Chapter 4. Several bad ideas regarding banking, monetary, and fiscal policy have been responsible for much of the economic distress of the past century. They were largely responsible for the Great Depression and the thirty-year inflation cycle that began in the mid-1960s. Their disappearance adds much to our optimistic outlook.

Of course, the very nature of government problem solving precludes the kind of excellent performance we would like to see. Government decisions in democracies are always a product of compromises (often defective ones) between competing interests. Compromises are usually slow in coming, sometimes dreadfully slow. Nevertheless, government decision making should be far better than in the Very Old Economy of the first half of the twentieth century or the Old Economy of the second half of that century.

No matter how much we wish it were so, market economies *cannot* run entirely on automatic pilot. Neither adequate aggregate demand nor intense structural competition occur automatically. They must be managed by government (including central banks). The management of aggregate demand after centuries of neglect (with unfortunate consequences) is now generally accepted. Monetary controls are the chosen tools, but the use of supplementary fiscal tools, though often cumbersome in their application, is gaining acceptance. The application of fiscal stimulation can be improved. Unprotected structural competition is often self-destructive. Monopoly is a frequent product of intense competition. Competitors try to reduce competition by collusion or merger.

New problems always arise. Many of them must be solved by governments. Therefore, the accuracy of medium-and long-term forecasts often depends on a proper appraisal of the problem-solving capabilities of governments. As deficient as these government capabilities now seem to be, the conditions for improving them as described in this report are far better than they have ever been before.

CULTURE WARS IN THE NEW ECONOMY

Culture wars are a raucous feature of New Economy societies. What are they? Every society must have devices to manage human behavior in order to stay functional. Management devices include formal laws and regulations together with informal customs and traditions. Culture wars are conflicts over behavior patterns and the nature of those management devices. In the United States, the culture wars are waged over issues such as these that have been linked to the culture wars on the Internet: abortion, gay rights, morality, struggle to define America, religion, political correctness, violence in movies, prostitution, drugs, affirmative action, feminism, crime deterrence, freedom of speech, and penal policy. At the international level, the conflict between Muslims and non-Muslims overwhelmingly dominates the culture wars at this time.

The New Economy intensifies culture wars in many ways:

- Globalization throws incompatible cultures more and more into contact with one another, setting the stage for increased conflict.
- Spread of democracy and its accompanying behavioral freedoms often makes for increased conflict. People living under authoritarian regimes that lay down rigid rules of conduct simply do not have the power to change behavioral patterns. Widespread debate is generally useless if not prohibited. Culture wars are less pervasive.
- Rapid technological change requires continued adjustments to behavior patterns upsetting established traditions. For example, modern technology has brought a large proportion of women into the labor force, thereby impacting most aspects of family life and relations between men and women.
- Increasing discretionary income expands opportunity to engage in a much wider range of activities increasing the diversity of human behavior and the diversity of interests that generate conflict.

Which cultural traits will survive the culture wars? Modern technology has decreed that we must live and work together in large groups with complex interrelationships. The ability to live and work together without disruptive conflict is, therefore, one of the most precious characteristics any society can possess. Those cultural traits that facilitate efficient and harmonious interrelationships will ultimately win out in the new world of competition among countries, governments, and cultures. Irregularly advancing New Economy conditions will provide the funding, incentives, and knowledge necessary to improve our ability to devise better formal and informal ways to manage human behavior patterns. Surely expanded research and experimentation should be able to come up with far superior answers to managing mundane aspects of human behavior such as drug addiction.

But many will argue that trends in crime, family dissolution, violence, and so on indicate a deterioration of our ability to maintain a harmonious society. They suggest that under the freedom provided by democracy and increasing wealth human nature is such that we will retreat from the personal responsibilities necessary for a harmonious, stable, productive society. Some suggest that the culture wars have already been lost. Perhaps so. But the full impact of recent trends has not been fully demonstrated. Trends may be reversed. And traits that have won the first few battles may not win the wars.

Which cultural traits will fail? No cultural trait clearly incompatible with modernization or with the forces we have described that are making modernization possible will survive unchanged. Some will survive for a while, but those that seriously impede the attraction of capital investment or the expansion of education are doomed to ultimate failure.

Culture wars will be a continuing, perhaps intensifying, aspect of the New Economy. Nevertheless, the capital-attraction requirement of modernization will keep most culture wars from escalating into real war. Peace is necessary to attract capital investment. How will this work out in today's conflict between Muslims and non-Muslims?

Muslims dream of becoming great as they once were. The more extreme among them believe that greatness can be achieved by militancy and by the adoption of a rigid form of Islam's Sharia law aided by a generous helping of divine intervention. This approach will continue to fail. Eventually Muslims must learn that greatness nowadays can be achieved only by providing an environment conducive to the attraction of capital investment. How will Muslims learn that lesson?

The fall of the Berlin Wall leading to the collapse of the Soviet Union delivered a near-fatal blow to the socialist doctrine. Dare we hope that the tragic events of September 11,

2001, might have a similar impact on extreme Islam? Just as the fall of the Berlin Wall led to the exposure of the pathetic performance of socialism in the Soviet Union, so also did 9/11 lead to the exposure of the hideous performance of a Muslim theocracy in Afghanistan. Bad examples are wonderful guides to future policy decisions.

Indications are proliferating that Muslims are learning. Saudi Arabia, the spiritual, financial, and historic center of Islam, has looked into the abyss revealed by 9/11 and has apparently begun backing away from past policies. The arrival of a genuine, economically viable Palestinian state will likely encourage many Muslim countries to abandon old ideas and join the struggle to modernize by attracting capital investment. That could be one of the most beneficial events of our time. Muslims make up a fifth of the world's population.

Progress in Meeting the Demand for More Compassionate Competitive Markets

A competitive market can be harsh. If left entirely alone, it can be brutal. Every advanced country on Earth has taken steps to soften the results of competitive markets. Methods include progressive income taxes, public-financed education, labor unions, antitrust laws, welfare programs, retirement plans, health insurance, environmental controls, disability benefits, price controls, and trade protection. Every single one of these approaches to soften the results of competition has at one time or another been abused with a negative impact on human welfare. Nevertheless, elements of most of those programs are useful and will certainly continue.

We have suggested more than once in this report that intensifying problems such as aging populations, the growing complexity of human society, and a widening gap between highly talented and less talented people will increase the demand for programs that soften the results of competitive markets. With such programs already taking between a quarter and a half of GDP in various countries, an increase in demand will put extreme pressure on the funding of such programs. Those countries that can meet these demands most efficiently, without detracting from the competition and incentives that make a market work properly, will take the lead in the struggle for wealth, power, and prestige. *One might argue that this is becoming the central economic problem of modern countries.* Governments at all levels — towns, cities, counties, states, and nations — are constantly facing this problem. They are competing with one another to solve the problem and learning from one another. That is the ideal condition for problem solving. Progress should be expected.

The Need for Valid Optimism

To convert an economy from government management to management by competition in the marketplace is a daunting task. A whole population must be reeducated. A great many qualified competitors must arise in business, labor, and the professions with the capital tools necessary to become effective. Prejudices must change. Many old habits have to be modified. New legal systems are required. Governments must abandon old practices and learn new regulatory responsibilities.

In view of the extreme and time-consuming difficulty of making the conversion, the progress made around the world *in just the last decade or two* must be viewed as phenomenal. China, to a lesser degree India, part of Latin America, Russia, Eastern Europe — countries containing more than half the world's population — have made enormous strides, (considering the difficulties involved). When mistakes have been made and difficulties have arisen, these countries have generally moved further toward market competition rather than falling back toward government management.

Although the New Economy twenty-first-century outlook is brilliant as compared with the Old Economy twentieth century, to declare victory now may be a bit premature. Yet, powerful new and intensifying competition is driving the acceleration of knowledge discovery and invention. It is also driving the governments of the world to create environments friendly to free markets and free democratic societies. These ongoing movements warrant the expectation of a gradually improving twenty-first century, eventually becoming far more pleasant than any extended period of time for which we have record. Overoptimism is deadly. Valid optimism is necessary to keep the struggle alive. Counsels of despair should be avoided. The wind is at our backs.

Chapter 8

NEW ECONOMY
STOCK MARKET VALUATIONS

The stock market has become an important driver of economic activity. Its fluctuations are often due to changing perceptions of the real value of stocks. Therefore, the analyses of the nature and durability of the New Economy presented in this report would not be complete without an analysis of stock market valuations under New Economy conditions. This chapter has been left until last because it uses the analyses provided throughout the report.

The stock market bubble of the late 1990s was clearly a consequence of an overly optimistic view of the financial implications of the New Economy. Could a reaction to the painful bursting of that bubble create a misinterpretation in the opposite direction? What stock market valuations are justified by our expectation of a continuation of New Economy characteristics of rapid productivity growth, low unemployment coexisting with low inflation, and mild, infrequent recessions?

All factors that influence stock prices operate through one or more of the following three measures:

- corporate revenue
- profit margins on revenue
- price-earnings (PE) ratios

These three measures may be either anticipated or realized. We shall attempt to forecast the three measures to estimate the long-term value of the Standard and Poor's stock index (S&P 500).

How Fast Will Corporate Revenue Grow?

Corporate revenue grows on average about one-quarter percentage point faster than *nominal* GDP. How fast will nominal GDP grow? Start with a probable average growth in employment of about 1¼ percent a year, a growth rate that assumes continued high immigration. (Of course employment will grow much faster for two or three years during recovery from the 2001 recession). Add 2½ percent a year average improvement in productivity (output per hour worked). As described in Chapter 3, a 2½ percent annual growth in *business* productivity is highly probable due to the Federal Reserve's commitment to maintain a low average inflation rate, and to the likely continuation of the past relationship between the productivity growth rate and the inflation rate as measured by the CPI. Adding productivity growth to employment growth results in 3¾ percent a year increase in *real* GDP. Then add 2 percent for inflation as measured by the GDP deflator. The sum of the real GDP and inflation growth rates provides an expected average increase of about 5¾ percent a year in *nominal* GDP after a more rapid surge during recovery to full employment. Corporate revenues growing about one-quarter percentage point faster, should grow about 6 percent a year.

In its efforts to contain inflation, the Federal Reserve will likely target the CPI because so many variables, including the social security escalator, are tied to that index and because it gets so much publicity. We have suggested that an average CPI inflation rate of 2½ percent will be achieved. But the GDP deflator in recent years has grown on average about half a percentage point slower than the CPI. Therefore, we have estimated that the deflator will increase about 2 percent a year. We must use the deflator to convert real GDP to nominal GDP.

A 3¾ percent average real growth rate is only moderately faster than the average 3.45 percent growth since 1950, but it is appreciably faster than the 3.10 percent growth since 1970. Actually we believe real growth may be even a little faster than 3¾ percent. Our justifications are an expected acceleration of knowledge discovery and invention (described in Chapter 1) and the intensification of competition (described in Chapter 2), which together will lead to a rapid improvement in productivity. Also (as described in Chapter 4), by shedding a number of bad ideas that have plagued our economy in the past, the monetary, fiscal, and banking authorities will be able to do a much better job of managing aggregate demand than they did in the Old Economy of the last fifty years. This improved capability will prevent the return of the stubborn inflation trends that have in the past precipitated serious corrective restraint on the growth rate. It will also provide sufficient demand to keep business activity strong enough to avoid both deep depressions and extended periods of slow growth.

How Much of the 6 Percent Increase in Corporate Revenue Will Be Retained as Profit?

Chart 8.1 shows profit margins *on revenue* for domestic U.S. nonfinancial corporations since 1959 as published in the monthly *Survey of Current Business*. What can we learn from this chart? Fluctuations have been spectacular and therefore have had an overwhelming impact on short-term changes in corporate profits. This volatility of profit margins makes profit margin projections both important and difficult.

Chart 8.1. Profit margin, domestic nonfinancial corporations.* Source: Survey of Current Business, Bureau of Economic Analysis.

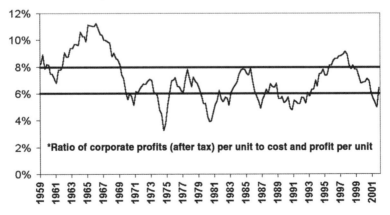

The great bull market of the 1990s was substantially abetted by an approximate 50 percent rise in profit margins from

1993 to 1997. This increase in profit margins, applied to rapidly growing corporate revenues, led to an annual growth in profits for several years of around 15 percent, encouraging widespread absurd forecasts that profits and the stock market would continue to rise at that pace for many years. It was a major factor behind the stock market bubble.

Granted that margins will continue to fluctuate, can an *average*, or "normal," rate for margins be forecast for the coming decade, and if so, how wide will fluctuations be around that average? If an average level for margins can be predicted, then stock prices reflecting margins far below that level can be looked on as a buying opportunity, and stock prices reflecting margins far above that level can be a warning to sell. What determines profit margins? Profits are a residual. They are what is left over after all costs are deducted from revenue. Being a residual, profits are knocked about by often unpredictable and uncontrollable changes in all items of revenue and cost involved in a business operation. Those items include quantities and prices of items sold, as well as cost of wages, worker benefits, materials, energy, taxes, and so on. Corporate management often requires considerable time to adjust to these changes in revenue and costs in order to achieve their target profit margins. Therefore, profits and profit margins fluctuate widely as economic conditions change.

Of all the *broad* factors that push profit margins around, *capacity utilization* and *changes in real GDP* are generally most important. Why does capacity utilization affect profit margins? As described earlier, when output drops below capacity, below-capacity competition becomes more vigorous, putting pressure on profit margins. Also, companies are forced to spread fixed costs over the smaller output, thus increasing unit costs and reducing profit margins. As for changes in *real* GDP, rapid growth obviously makes the maintenance of selling prices above costs (which tend to lag) easier to achieve, leading to high margins.

Wall Street analysts frequently use the term "pricing power." This is a euphemism for the ability to maintain satisfactory profit margins. In 2002, reports of the inability to maintain adequate pricing power were almost continuous.

This should not be surprising since the two broad factors that usually dominate profit margins were weak—capacity utilization and growth in real GDP. When these two factors strengthen, pricing power will return to more normal levels. What are these levels?

Is it likely that the high margins above 8 percent shown in the chart for the 1960s will be repeated? That was an extraordinary period of rapid growth, high capacity utilization (low below-capacity competition), and, through part of the period, *accelerating inflation*. Rapid economic growth will surely reappear, but if it is accompanied by the low below-capacity competition of that period with its rapid inflation, Federal Reserve inflation-stabilizing policy will quickly kick in, the economy will slow, and profit margins will decline. The very high profit margins of 1963-69 will not likely be repeated, at least for any prolonged period. Much the same can be said for the profit margins slightly above 8 percent in 1996-97. That was also a period of rapid growth in real GDP, but below-capacity competition was significantly stronger (capacity utilization lower) than in the 1960s.

As the chart shows, the other extreme (low profit margins, below 6 percent) has been associated with recessions, very slow growth, and strong below-capacity competition. If we are correct that the Federal Reserve, with a bit of help from fiscal authorities, can continue to keep recessions mild and infrequent, we can rule out the possibility of profit margins *averaging* below 6 percent and confine the expected average profit margin range to between 6 and 8 percent, still an unpleasantly wide latitude.

Perhaps that likely two-percentage-point range of expected average profit margins can be narrowed a bit. We have argued in this report that several of the forces underlying New Economy *structural* competition will continue. Therefore, the productivity and real GDP growth rates will continue stronger than the dismal growth rates that persisted through the inflation cycle from the late 1960s to the early 1990s. It follows that profit margins should be higher. Likewise, strong structural competition will require less below-capacity competition to restrain inflation, also leading to higher profit margins than prevailed in that thirty year period. Therefore, we suggest that the average profit margin for the coming decade or two will be somewhere in the 7 to 8 percent range, using the data supplied by the *Survey of Current Business*. From the low level of the 2001 recession, profit margins should rise to this range. From then on, corporate profits should grow at about the same average rate as corporate revenue, about 6 percent a year. That 7-to-8 percentage point range is not meant to convey a sense of great precision. It is just saying that average profit margins are likely to be higher than in the inflation cycle of the 1970s, 1980s, and even the early 1990s. Furthermore, as we shall shortly explain, sometime in the future high stock market valuations (PE ratios) may bring higher levels of investment that will hold margins a little below the 7-to-8 percent range for an extended period.

Other published records of profit margins on revenue vary somewhat from the one we have used. Yet they do not impair our main conclusion that profit margins in the coming years will average considerably higher than they did in the 1970s, 1980s, and early 1990s.

What Price-Earnings Ratio Will Prevail?

In forecasting PE ratios, we are forecasting how investors will value stocks. What price will investors pay (not *should* pay, but *will* pay) for the stream of earnings that they expect will be generated by the two factors already examined—the growth of revenue and the share of that revenue to be retained as profit? This problem requires complex analyses involving several topics, especially an estimation of the growth of S&P 500 per share earnings needed to put a value on that index. We can best introduce this subject by making three general observations:

- Most long-term investors have only one basic choice. They can invest in either stocks or bonds. Therefore, the valuation of stocks depends heavily on the valuation of bonds, the alternative investment. Investors will pay less for stocks if bonds are attractive. Valuing bonds is also difficult. Bond investment, like stock investment, has been hazardous. For example, bonds suffered an irregular thirty-five year bear market from World War II to 1981 as the Federal Reserve quit pegging long-term interest rates and as the inflation cycle unfolded.

- The advent of New Economy conditions has improved the outlook for bonds more than it has improved the outlook for stocks. Serious, sporadic inflation was one of the important problems of the Old Economy. The taming of inflation has been one of the accomplishments of the New Economy. As the fear of accelerating inflation that had haunted the bond market for decades has diminished, the outlook for bonds has greatly improved. The outlook for *stocks* has also improved as fears of deep depression have receded and the incidence of recession has lessened, removing much of the fear of large extended declines in profits. More rapid growth is also improving the outlook for stocks. But these improvements will be offset by a slower inflation rate. Inflation, by itself, *over the long term* is good for stocks since it speeds revenue growth, to which corporate profits are closely tied. Even with a more rapid growth of *real* GDP, the slower growth of inflation will yield a growth in *nominal* GDP about $1\frac{1}{2}$ percentage points less than the growth from 1950 to 2000.

- The extreme difficulty of determining long-term valuations of both stocks and bonds has turned a great many investors (at least to some degree) into short-term market timers. Investor concern is directed heavily toward predicting events that will impact the markets in the coming quarter or coming year. Even most dedicated long-term investors use short-term forecasting as an auxiliary tool. We will discuss short-term market valuation in a later section. Most of the following analysis is directed toward determining long-term valuations.

We suggest that U.S. Treasury obligations with ten year maturities will yield, on average, about $5\frac{1}{2}$ percent over the coming decade, substantially more than late 2002 yields of $3\frac{3}{4}$ percent. Therefore, we believe that ten year notes at late 2002 yields were overvalued on a two-to five-year time horizon.

Total U.S. corporate profits should grow about 6 percent a year after a more rapid initial recovery from the 2001 recession. *Per-share* profits on the S&P 500 will likely grow at about the same rate. In addition, investors will receive an approximate $1\frac{1}{2}$ percent annual dividend yield for a total return of about $7\frac{1}{2}$ percent.

The PE ratio on the S&P 500 should *average* about 18 or 20 (on full employment earnings) during the coming decade, somewhat below the 22.6 average of the 1990s but well above the 15.5 average of the past half century. If these forecasts materialize, the S&P 500 was significantly undervalued on a two-to five-year time horizon at the late 2002 price of 875.

No one should believe that this forecast is meant to be precise. We are aware of several things that could upset the forecast substantially. But at least we are attempting what we believe to be an essential approach—valuing stocks and bonds under New Economy conditions of rapid productivity growth, low unemployment coexistent with low inflation, and mild, infrequent recessions, rather than going back a whole century and just taking averages of various metrics that prevailed under the Very Old Economy.

We think this approach is necessary because we find it difficult to believe that PE ratios or the relative investment performance of bonds and stocks that prevailed during the first half of the twentieth century (the Very Old Economy) have much relevance to their performance in the New Economy. The Very Old Economy was burdened by primitive financial systems with their frequent money panics, two world wars, the Great Depression, and a collapse of the international trading system engendered by the protectionist experiment of the Smoot-Hawley tariff. Even the second half of the twentieth century (the Old Economy) did not provide useful evidence of investment performance that we might expect in the New Economy. It was burdened by the Cold War, the long inflation cycle from 1965 to 1995, inadequate structural competition over much of the period, and the stultifying effects of the dying but still prevalent socialist dogma around much of the world. We must now attempt to justify our forecasts under the New Economy conditions that we have projected.

Is Our Forecast of Bond Interest Rates Correct?

U.S. government bond interest rates have two components: first, the real interest rate necessary to induce lenders to give up the use of their money for a period of time, and second, an inflation premium to protect lenders from losses due to a possible decline in the purchasing power of their money during the life of the loan. (Corporate bonds bear an additional premium to cover risk of default.) Massive swings in the inflation premium required by bond buyers have accounted for most of the wide fluctuations in interest rates over the past half century.

We have only meager direct evidence of bond buyers' demands for *real* interest rates. Charts showing real interest rates as the difference between nominal interest rates and concurrent inflation rates are not correct. *Real* interest rates are the difference between nominal interest rates and *expected* inflation rates which often vary widely from concurrent inflation rates. For example, for a few years after the sharp drop in the inflation rate following the inflationary 1970s a six-to-eight percentage-point spread prevailed between the ten-year Treasury note yield and the inflation rate. This spread did not represent the *real* interest rate. It represented the real interest rate plus a premium to protect the bond buyer from a possible return to the high inflation of the 1970s.

Since 1997, the U.S. Treasury has issued ten-year notes with inflation-protected principle and interest. Therefore, the interest rates these obligations carry are real interest rates. Yields have averaged somewhat more than 3 percent. However, these U.S. Treasury obligations are new and unseasoned and have limited liquidity. Therefore, we assume that inflation-protected U.S. notes or bonds with liquidity equal to that of other U.S. notes and bonds would have yielded somewhat less. The inflation-protected securities apparently indicated that the real interest rate during this five-year period for notes with greater liquidity would have been about 3 percent.

Another indication of real interest rates comes from U.S. experience in the early 1960s, the only other period of relative economic stability and low inflation expectations in the past half century. During that period, government bond interest rates averaged about 4 percent. CPI inflation averaged about 1 percent, and surveys indicated that people expected that that low inflation rate would continue. The real interest rate demanded by lenders during the early 1960s was apparently somewhere near 3 percent. These two pieces of evidence lead us to project that the real interest rate component will average about 3 percent under New Economy conditions.

The required inflation premium has been declining irregularly since the early 1980s as the memory of the pain of serious inflation has faded and as Federal Reserve policy has demonstrated a clear intent to avoid accelerating inflation in the future. We therefore estimate that the future inflation premium will average about $2\frac{1}{2}$ percent, the likely Federal Reserve target for the CPI. The future bond (ten year note) yield should average about $5\frac{1}{2}$ percent, including the real interest rate and inflation premium.

Any expected divergence from this average yield would have a major impact on the PE ratio that investors would pay for stocks. A one-percentage-point error in our interest rate estimate could change the average price paid by stock investors and thereby change by 2 or 3 points the 18-to-20 PE ratio we have projected. Clearly, analysts must be aware of the considerable uncertainty injected into PE forecasting by the difficulty of projecting bond yields.

Although we have projected a continued New Economy average *real* interest rate of 3 percent in the United States, we recognize that it may change due to a number of developments that could affect the supply of, and demand for, investable funds. Interest rates will be determined more and more on a worldwide basis. Huge amounts of investment in plant and equipment will be required as modernization spreads around the world. The traditional high Asian savings rate may succumb to the temptation of American-style consumer credit. Governments may change their attitude toward deficit financing. None of these factors can be predicted with confidence. Nevertheless, future changes in interest rates due to changes in real interest rates will surely be mild compared to the wild swings resulting from past shifts in the required inflation premium. *Short-term* fluctuations will continue as the Federal Reserve manipulates interest rates to influence aggregate demand.

How Fast Will S&P 500 Earnings Grow?

We have projected an average 6 percent annual growth in total U.S. corporate profits after an initial more rapid surge accompanying full recovery from the 2001 recession. How do we get from that projection to the projection of per share earnings on the S&P 500 that we must have to value that index? We get there only with considerable difficulty, but we must try.

We start with the simple approach of comparing the two profit measures over the past half century. From 1950 to 2000, S&P 500 per-share earnings grew just 0.22 percentage points faster than total U.S. corporate profits but 0.64 percentage points more slowly than total U.S. profits with IVA and CCA adjustments. Can we, therefore, forecast that the S&P 500 per-share earnings growth will approximate the 6 percent growth rate that we have forecast for total U.S. corporate profits (after the post recession surge)? We do, but with many warnings of factors that could upset that relationship.

First, the two growth rates diverge considerably over short periods. From year to year the two profit measures differ substantially in their growth rates, sometimes moving in different directions. From decade to decade there has been considerable variation. Of the past five decades, the 1950s and

96

1960s showed relative growth rates reasonably similar to the average of the entire fifty years. But in the 1970s total U.S. corporate profits grew almost three percentage points faster than the S&P 500 per-share earnings. That was an unusual decade of accelerating inflation and somewhat slower real growth. Then in the following decade the two profit growth rates reversed. S&P 500 per-share earnings grew almost three percentage points faster than total U.S. corporate profits. That was a decade of decelerating inflation and more rapid growth. In the 1990s S&P 500 earnings grew a little more slowly than total U.S. profits. One must expect variation from average growth rates over fairly long periods.

The two measures of profit cover different corporate universes. U.S. corporate profits cover all corporations, large and small, public and private. The S&P 500 index covers only five hundred large companies, as many as 10 percent of which are changed each year. The two measures are computed under different accounting standards. Tax returns are the basis for U.S. corporate profits, but they are adjusted in many ways to bring them somewhat closer to agreement with financial accounting. Financial accounting is the basis for S&P 500 earnings. Accounting standards may change. Many of the S&P 500 corporations have extensive international operations, and their earnings are especially vulnerable to changing foreign exchange rates.

The greatest worry lies in the important dilution factor. When additional shares are issued by the S&P 500 companies, profits *per share* are diluted, and per-share earnings grow more slowly. At least five factors have affected per-share dilution over the past half century and may affect it in the future.

- *Dividend pay-out ratio.* Dividends increase quite steadily, but since profits fluctuate substantially from year to year, the ratio of dividends to profit also fluctuates substantially. The pay-out ratio has dropped from an average of 57 percent for the first five years of the 1950s to an average of 39 percent during the last five years of the 1990s. That means that an additional 18 percent of earnings was retained for corporate purposes, thereby reducing the need for raising funds by issuing new stock. Per-share earnings dilution was avoided to that extent, and per-share earnings growth was enhanced. If the much-discussed tax deductibility of dividends is enacted, dividends will surely be increased, requiring greater stock issuance, increasing dilution, and slowing per-share earnings growth. That, of course, will be offset to the stockholder by greater dividend return. In contrast, *if all dividends were to end*, the need for equity financing would slow, stock buy-backs would increase, the net dilution factor would drop, and the rate of growth of S&P 500 earnings would increase, probably reaching our projected total return of $7\frac{1}{2}$ percent including earnings growth and reinvested dividends.

- *Debt-to-capital ratios.* Corporate debt has increased in recent years as a percentage of capital structures. Of course, greater use of debt is warranted under more stable New Economy conditions, especially as the inflation premium included in interest rates has declined. Increased debt financing reduced the need for equity financing and thus held down the issuance of dilutive shares. Debt financing may have gone about as far as it can go and may, therefore, not act as a restraint on dilutive stock issuance in the coming years.

- *Stock options.* The extensive use of stock options in the 1990s added to stock issuance, increasing dilution and slowing the growth of per-share earnings. Part of that stock issuance was offset by stock buy-backs. We expect that the use of stock options will decline.

- *Expansion rate.* A more rapid expansion of productive capacity requires greater capital expenditures and greater capital resources, often requiring greater issuance of stock and increasing per-share earnings dilution. The rapid expansion of productive capacity (along with stock options) probably accounted for the bulk of the dilution of per-share earnings in the late 1990s.

- *Capital-output ratio.* If capital requirements increase faster than output (capital-output ratio increases), a greater demand for funds will arise. Therefore, an increase in the capital-output ratio would require greater dilutive stock issuance and slow the growth of per-share earnings. A decline in the capital-output ratio would do the opposite. In the coming age of accelerating technological change, with increased capital often used to replace labor, changes in the capital-output ratio are unpredictable. Ratios will surely vary from industry to industry.

All this detail has been supplied as a caution against the mechanical use of the past relationship between the S&P 500 and total U.S. corporate profits. That is especially true for short periods. An analyst must be alert for changes in each of the above-described factors.

In spite of all the factors just described that can produce divergence between the growth of total U.S. corporate profits and S&P 500 per-share earnings, we still expect that the two measures will grow on average at roughly the same rate, about 6 percent a year. Apparently, over the past fifty years, *total* S&P 500 earnings grew faster than U.S. corporate profits, but the issuance of more shares diluted *per-share* earnings which grew at about the same rate as total U.S. corporate profits. That is roughly what happened from 1988 to 2000, the only period for which we have *total* earnings for the S&P 500. Those earnings grew much faster than total U.S. corporate profits, but the dilution factor due to the perceived need for unusual capital spending and stock options was so great that S&P 500 *per share* earnings grew just a little faster than total U.S. corporate profits.

And that brings us to a shorthand approach to forecasting S&P 500 per-share earnings. They should grow, on average, about the same as *nominal* GDP after the initial post-recession surge. Anyone who wants to attempt a more precise forecast than this must go through all the factors we have described that impact the S&P 500 earnings growth, including the difficult-to-predict dilution factor. Such an effort is warranted for short-term earnings projections. We have suggested that under the more stable New Economy conditions, nominal GDP will be easier to predict on a long-term basis than under Old Economy or Very Old Economy conditions. Therefore, long-term growth of S&P 500 per share earnings should also be easier to predict. That is what we need for long-term stock valuations.

S&P 500 PER-SHARE TOTAL RETURN

To our projected 6-percent growth of per share earnings on the S&P 500 we must add an expected dividend to get *total* per-share return. After stock prices and profits recover from the 2001 recession, the S&P 500 should show a dividend yield of about 1½ percent of the index price. Dividends during the ensuing years should grow on average pretty much in line with corporate earnings and corporate revenue. Therefore a dividend of 1½ percent of the price of stocks should be expected each year to add to the expected 6 percent earnings growth, yielding an average total return of 7½ percent including reinvested dividends.

SUMMARY OF OUR PROJECTIONS

Here, then, is a summary of our projections of interest rates and earnings for the coming decade or two.

	Percent
Long-term Treasury bonds (notes)	
Expected average real interest rate	3
Expected average inflation premium (change in CPI)	+ 2½
Expected average interest rate on U.S. Treasury ten-year notes	5½
Common stocks	
Growth in employment	1¼
Productivity growth rate per hour worked	+ 2½

100

Expected growth rate real GDP	$3^3/_4$
Expected inflation rate for GDP deflator (a half percentage point less than CPI)	+ 2
Expected growth rate of nominal GDP	$5^3/_4$
Expected growth rate of corporate revenue (a quarter percentage point faster than nominal GDP)	6
Expected growth rate of total U.S. corporate profits after initial surge during recovery from 2001 recession (same growth rate as corporate revenue)	6
S&P 500 per share earnings, (same growth rate as total U.S. corporate profits)	6
Dividend Yield	+ $1^1/_2$
Total per-share return on the S&P 500	$7^1/_2$

COMPARING RETURNS ON STOCKS AND BONDS

We are now ready to compare an expected long-term $7^1/_2$ percent total return per share on the S&P 500 stock index with an expected $5^1/_2$ percent yield on bonds. Which is the better investment?

Stocks have a decided tax advantage. Bond interest is taxed each year at regular rates. Appreciation on stocks is taxed at the lower capital gains rate and is deferred until stocks are sold. This is a substantial advantage to tax-paying investors but not to most retirement funds and other non-tax-paying entities.

Stocks are said to be riskier than bonds and therefore it is often claimed that their return should provide a risk premium over bond yields. What is this risk in stock investment? Over long periods stocks have outperformed bonds, and we are projecting that they will continue to do so although to a lesser degree than in the past. The risks of stock investment lie in the volatility of stock prices and in the uncertainty of the size of their long-term performance advantage over bonds.

As for volatility, stock prices are generally much more volatile than bond prices. This will be especially true in the New Economy low-inflation environment, which will reduce the volatility of bond prices. To dedicated long-term investors, stock volatility may be just an inconvenience. But to investors with an investment horizon under ten years, it can be a serious problem. Stock prices may be low just when the funds are needed.

Errors in predicting the size of the superior long-term performance over bonds could be either a plus or a minus for stock investment. Nevertheless, they add an element of uncertainty that many investors do not care to face, and thus may militate against stock investment.

The relative importance of the tax and risk factors cannot be weighted precisely. Therefore, we suggest that the two may balance out in the mind of the "average investor". And that leads to a simple comparison of an expected bond yield of about $5\frac{1}{2}$ percent and an expected total return on stocks of about $7\frac{1}{2}$ percent. To a long-term investor the decision seems obvious. A thousand dollars invested in stocks at a $7\frac{1}{2}$ percent total return would in ten years amount to 1.21 times the amount invested in bonds at a $5\frac{1}{2}$ percent return, in twenty years to 1.46 times, in fifty years to 2.56 times, and in a hundred years to 6.54 times. For many investors the tax advantage could be added to the outperformance of stock investment. But the important problem remains. We must translate the relative growth rates into PE ratios that investors will pay for stocks.

Estimating how investors will value stocks is not easy. A constant PE ratio of 13.3 on a $7\frac{1}{2}$ percent total return would provide a $7\frac{1}{2}$ percent average return on stocks. But since this would likely be preferred to a $5\frac{1}{2}$ percent yield on bonds, investors would probably bid up the price of stocks to a higher earnings multiple. But how much? The exact PE that investors will be willing to pay for a specific growth in earnings depends on two things: *how much confidence they have in the relative reliability of earnings and interest rate projections and how far into the future they expect that earnings-interest rate differential to persist.* The more confidence they have in the earnings and interest rate projections and the longer they expect the differential to persist, the higher the PE they will be willing to pay.

Our interest rate and earnings growth rate projections would warrant an extremely high PE ratio if expected to continue for a very long time, say, seventy-five or a hundred years. That PE, based on full-employment earnings, would be well over 50. One highly publicized forecast made in 1999 using a different mathematical approach indicated that a PE ratio of 100 would be appropriate.[ix] But high PE valuations have built-in limitations. As PE ratios rise, stocks take on some of the attributes of money that can be printed cheaply. New stock issues are used for buying almost anything at almost any price: companies, technologies, star executives, employees, plant and equipment, real estate, bonds, sometimes even politicians. And this activates the dreaded dilution factor described earlier that slows the growth in per-share earnings. It also leads to rapid expansion of capacity, which intensifies competition and drives down profit margins. Furthermore, it tempts corporate executives to use deceptive and illegal techniques to increase earnings to boost stock prices, making their cheaply printed stock certificates more valuable. This is a reasonably accurate description of the sequence of events that unfolded in the last half of the 1990s, bringing the bubble to an end.

It is virtually impossible mathematically to determine an S&P 500 PE ratio that will represent the present value of a stream of earnings considered to be growing *endlessly* at a rate significantly higher than the return on the alternative bond investment. Also, small errors in the expected growth rate of S&P 500 per-share earnings or in the future average return on bonds will make a considerable difference to the present value of stocks even for shorter time horizons.

FACTORS THAT WILL AFFECT PE RATIOS IN THE NEXT DECADE OR TWO

• Memory of the pain from the breaking of the recent

bubble will tend for a time to suppress PE ratios on full-employment earnings well below the 30-plus ratios of the very late 1990s and even below the 22.6 average of the entire 1990s decade.

- The difficulty of making long-term projections will lead investors to base PE valuations on short-term projections. The so-called Federal Reserve valuation model (and many other valuation models) puts great emphasis on existing conditions and projections for just the coming year. Emphasis on short-term valuation criteria will inevitably produce considerable volatility.

- If our projections of a continuation of New Economy characteristics are correct (and that is the critical question), stock investment will outperform bond investment irregularly for several years. During recovery from the 2001 recession we may see double-digit earnings growth for two or three years. This will gradually encourage investment in stocks, and PE ratios will likely rise fairly soon to the 18-to-20 range based on post-recession earnings. That range would be considered appropriate by some present-day short-term valuation models based on our expected average $5\frac{1}{2}$ percent yield on ten year notes. As memories of the bubble aftermath fade, PEs may rise somewhat higher.

- But PE ratios cannot rise indefinitely. In the next several years the economy will be operating most of the time near full employment. Rapid productivity growth combined with a growing labor force will keep real growth close to 4 percent a year. S&P 500 per-share earnings will be increasing on average near 6 percent a year, and dividend yields will be between 1 and 2 percent. We suspect that a growing conviction of the persistence of New Economy conditions will once again engender contagious optimism in the security markets. The difficulty of determining long-term stock valuations, the short-term emotional nature of markets, and the continuation of New Economy characteristics will ensure that sooner or later extreme valuations will be upon us. But then at some unknown point as PE ratios rise, cheaply printed stock certificates will once more gain some of the attributes of money, creating dilution sufficient to slow per share earnings growth and encouraging excessive investment that will drive down profit margins. Investment managers will always have to live in fear of these adverse consequences whenever high PE ratios prevail.

- Over the next several years the actual PE ratio is not likely to be determined mainly by mathematical efforts to arrive at the present value of the S&P 500 derived from long-term projections of future earnings and dividends. Nor is it likely to be determined by examination of historical records of PE ratios that prevailed under vastly differing conditions. It is more likely to be determined by the "animal spirits" engendered by views of the future of the U.S. and world economies That is why it is so important for investors to make a judgment about our view of the real New Economy and about other views that are more pessimistic or more optimistic than ours.

In early 2000 "animal spirits" were high. We were living in a wonderful New Economy. By the fall of 2002 spirits had crumpled. The term New Economy was seldom used, and when used was most often derided. If our New Economy analysis is correct, animal spirits should soon revive although for a time considerably subdued. Stock prices should respond accordingly.

AN OVERVIEW OF LONG-TERM INVESTING

- Two or three decades from now, a look back at this forecast will find most of the numbers wrong. Yet they are not likely to be as wrong as the forecasts that project far into the future the metrics from the primitive financial conditions of the Very Old Economy that prevailed in the first half of the twentieth century. The substantial outperformance of stocks over bonds under Very Old Economy conditions will surely be moderated.

105

Forecasts that project Very Old Economy PE ratios will likely prove to be too pessimistic. Forecasts based on the conviction that the New Economy is just an illusion will also likely be too pessimistic and fare worse than our projections.

• Unless a stock-investment program is well designed, the modest advantage of stock investment over bonds will be eaten up by high mutual fund management fees and/or trading commissions. The justification for the partial privatization of social security disappears under the realization that much of the modest long-term stock superiority can be frittered away by those management fees and brokerage commissions. Millions of unsophisticated social security investors would be especially vulnerable to this problem, often succumbing to the blandishments of high-impact TV advertising.

• Small errors (which are very likely to exist) in one or more of our projected factors controlling bond and stock prices may substantially increase or decrease the expected premium of stocks over bonds.

• As difficult as it is to estimate long-term stock and bond valuations, investors must somehow arrive at estimates in order to survive the constant noise of arguments as to whether stocks are too high or too low. Also, of course, long-term investors must protect themselves from wide emotional swings in market prices.

• The problem of coping with long-term valuation uncertainties will encourage a great many investors to continue emphasizing short-term investment considerations, a topic to which we will now turn.

THE SHORT-TERM NATURE OF TODAY'S MARKETS

We now have a few useful (and some not so useful) TV programs devoted to finance and investment. Respected money managers, analysts, journalists, and corporate executives appear on these programs. They demonstrate the most outstanding feature of today's markets. They are excessively oriented to the short term. Discussions mostly concern the question: What will the market, or an individual stock, or interest rates do next month or next quarter? Slight disappointments in earnings now cause major sell-offs in the market. Modest surprises in economic data produce wide market swings. This short-term orientation is not new, although it has been vastly intensified by the adoption and popularization of speculative vehicles such as options and futures contracts. Quick, short-term trading has been facilitated by electronic equipment and low commissions. The short-term orientation of markets is understandable. Long-term projections are difficult to make. And there is always the almost irresistible temptation to try to predict and profit from short-term swings in the markets. In hindsight, it looks so easy.

Examples of short-term oriented investors include those who buy a stock because they think it will go up within a year even though they believe it is overvalued on a longer-term basis, or perhaps they have no idea at all of what it is worth over a longer term. They also sell a stock because they think it will soon go down even though they believe it is worth more over a longer period.

Actually, short-term investing may be even more difficult than long-term investing. The short-term trader must predict not only short-term events but also (even more difficult) how other traders will respond to those events. And so the difficulties of both long- and short-term investing will ensure that our oddly labeled "efficient" market will continue to leave stock pricing on a short-term basis, subject to emotion, short-term trading, aggressive salesmen, momentum players, and poorly informed investors, all of whom have little interest in long-term valuations. Stock prices will continue to be volatile, leaving great opportunities for the perspicacious few who learn to profit from (or insulate themselves from) those poorly informed, emotional swings in the market.

Who are these perspicacious few? They include, most importantly, skilled long-term investors who examine individual companies carefully and say to themselves, "I don't know how well the stocks I have selected will perform this year, but I am convinced that their intrinsic value is substantially more than they are now selling for, and that sometime in the next year or two, their prices will rise to reflect that value." These long-term investors, of course, generally have some judgment as to likely near-term events and how they will impact the market, but that judgment is secondary to their judgment as to the longer-term intrinsic value of individual companies. Needless to say, these true long-term investors are highly skilled and have unusual mental and emotional discipline. Volatile markets, strongly impacted by short-term considerations and under the sway of powerful emotions, will frequently value many stocks badly, providing profitable investment opportunities for these long-term investors.

These emotional markets will also provide excellent opportunities to sell at substantial profits. This is not market timing. It is not predicting what the market will do this quarter or this year. It is merely recognizing that our volatile markets often price stocks far higher than they are really worth And, most important, *determining true long-term value for individual companies* is often easier than determining the true long-term value of, say, the S&P 500 index. To the long-term investor, wide emotional market swings are not just a problem. They are also an opportunity.

The perspicacious few also include those who admit they don't have the ability to judge the value of individual companies or to forecast short-term movements in the market. They also are not sure whom they can trust to do it for them. They buy the entire market through an index fund (with low management fees) and use the old-fashioned approach of investing the same dollar amount each month, thus insuring that they buy more shares when prices are low than when prices are high. Millions of investors have used this technique in their retirement accounts with great success when they have started early and continued the program for many years. In this case, "the perspicacious few" have turned out to be the perspicacious many.

Or perhaps they use the old-fashioned balanced fund, in which, say, 60 percent of investable assets are always held in stocks and 40 percent in bonds. Investors are thus forced to sell stocks when prices rise substantially and buy them when prices drop. This approach also requires a long period to be successful.

The perspicacious few include as well an unknown number of investors who have considerable ability to predict short-term events and appraise investor psychology. Some of these investors do very well, but some who think they have the necessary capabilities are just having a long and unusual run of good luck.

A few comments should be made at this time about the terms *value* investor and *growth* investor as currently used in financial jargon. The two types of investors are usually differentiated by the *types of stocks they buy*. Value investors are said to buy low PE, moderately growing, high asset, even dividend-paying stocks. Growth investors are said to buy stocks in presumably rapidly growing companies with high PEs, sometimes with no current earnings at all.

Defining investors by what they buy is a mistake. They should be defined by the *time horizon* involved in their investment decisions. Value investors can buy stocks in high PE, rapidly growing companies as long as their decision is based *not* on what the stock (or the market generally) will likely do this year, *not* on the fact that it has momentum or has grown rapidly in the past, but on the fact that it has a competitive advantage and other qualities that make it worth more than its current price. This is treacherous ground, but value investors miss great opportunities if they automatically rule out high PE companies. In the years to come the hunger for rapid growth will continue to be with us, and companies with growth potential only moderately higher than the $7\frac{1}{2}$ percent total return expected on the S&P 500 will command significantly higher PE ratios than the ratio for the market average.

****

In this chapter, we have emphasized the uncertainties involved in making financial forecasts. Many things can go wrong. But in this report as a whole, we have emphasized the important aspects of the New Economy that are likely to go *right*. The governments of the world will be forced by competition and the need to modernize to adopt those wonderful policies described in Chapter 7 that are necessary to attract capital investment. The changing nature and intensity of competition among private producers on a globalized basis will ensure a long-term acceleration of knowledge discovery and invention, leading to improved productivity and much greater wealth more evenly distributed among countries. The monetary authorities will be forced by suspicious bond investors to maintain a reasonably effective anti-inflation policy.

Of course, the path toward a globalized, competitive New Economy will not be smooth. The bumps and potholes along the way will make many wonder at times if we have lost our way. Hopes and fears induced by these bumps and potholes will be exaggerated in volatile financial markets, providing enticing opportunities for those with the mental discipline to see the emotional swings for what they are.

End Notes

[i] Alfred D. Stafford, "Is the Rate of Invention Declining?" *The American Journal of Sociology*, May 1956.

[ii] World Bank and Oxford University Press, *Globalization, Growth, and Poverty: Building An Inclusive World Economy*," 2002. See also *The Economist*, "Special Report on Globalization," February 2, 2002, p. 66.

[iii] Much of this discussion of the organization of R&D was taken from Hebert I. Fusfeld, *Industry's Future: Changing Patterns of Industrial Research*, Washington, D.C.: American Chemical Society, 1994.

[iv] Burton H. Klein, *Dynamic Economics*, Cambridge, MA: Harvard University Press, 1977; Burton H. Klein, *Prices, Wages, and Business Cycles: A Dynamic Theory*, New York: Pergamon Press, 1984: Burton H. Klien, "Making Luck and Necessity Go Hand in Hand," Mimeo from author, 1988.

[v] Lawrence M. Rausch, "Venture Capital Investment Trends in the U.S. and Europe", National Science Foundation, October 16, 1998.

[vi] William G. Shepherd, *The Economics of Industrial Organization*, Englewood Cliffs, N.J., Prentice-Hall, 1979.

[vii] *The Economist*, March 16, 2002, p. 16.

[iix] Thomas D. Hopkins, "The Costs of Federal Regulation," *Policy Analysis*, Washington, D.C. National Chamber Foundation, 1992; and "Costs of Regulation: Filling the Gaps," Report prepared for the Regulatory Information Service Center, August 1992.

[ix] James K. Glassman and Kevin A. Hassett, *Dow 36,000*, Three Rivers Press, 1999.